It Began with a Stubby

A Spiritual Awakening, Aussie Style

Darrell H. Poke

BALBOA.
PRESS

A DIVISION OF HAY HOUSE

Balboa Press books may be ordered through booksellers or by contacting:

Balboa Press
A Division of Hay House
1663 Liberty Drive
Bloomington, IN 47403
www.balboapress.com.au
1 (877) 407-4847

Because of the dynamic nature of the Internet, any web addresses or
links contained in this book may have changed since publication and
may no longer be valid. The views expressed in this work are solely those
of the author and do not necessarily reflect the views of the publisher,
and the publisher hereby disclaims any responsibility for them.

The author of this book does not dispense medical advice or prescribe the use
of any technique as a form of treatment for physical, emotional, or medical
problems without the advice of a physician, either directly or indirectly. The
intent of the author is only to offer information of a general nature to help you
in your quest for emotional and spiritual well-being. In the event you use any
of the information in this book for yourself, which is your constitutional right,
the author and the publisher assume no responsibility for your actions.

Any people depicted in stock imagery provided by Thinkstock are
models, and such images are being used for illustrative purposes only.
Certain stock imagery © Thinkstock.

Printed in the United States of America.

ISBN: 978-1-4525-1264-8 (sc)
ISBN: 978-1-4525-1265-5 (e)

Balboa Press rev. date: 01/03/2014

Contents

Introduction

It Began with a Stubby is Spiritual Awakening from someone else's perspective.

As I began to write my first book, I pondered the question, where does one begin writing a book about Spirituality when one comes to the realization, there's no beginning and no end to anything?

With the perception that life begins with the first breath and ends with the last, and like a journey, we plan the beginning; take action by going on the journey and return, end of journey.

So it must be with writing a book, starting with the first page and seemingly ending with the last.

There are many questions as to why I am writing this book, why Spirituality?

Why not fiction?

Why not an autobiography, why bother writing at all?

I am writing this book simply because I feel I am compelled to, I am driven to, this is a small part of my destiny, it's a journey of awakening which began consciously some twenty years ago becoming Spiritual has been a step by step to an ever increasing awakening, an understanding of our deeper mind, our subconscious mind, one brain, two minds.

Being raised as I thought at the time, an Atheist, to an awakening of the truth of perceived reality of life, a life which becomes truly amazing and magnificent as our minds open up to life as we come to know it, is truly awesome.

I like most heading down the Spiritual path all started somewhere, I was very sceptical in the beginning, but being of a practical and humble upbringing, I've removed all the scientific jargon and say it as I see it and explain it along with other points as I would during a normal discussion.

I've not dumbed it down for any intent or purpose nor am I writing it to try and gain a thesis for a diploma or master's degree, I am just an everyday knock about run of the mill person bringing what I have learned along the way, to the readers in the hope it can touch someone enough for them to do something similar, and one person at a time, we can make the world an even more amazing place than it already is.

The book is also not a large book; it is also written in bite size chunks so as not to overload the reader with too much information and can be put down at any time without having to read mega pages just to end the chapter.

Having said that, there is some repetitive information which is all linked to help the reader build new synapses or anchor points in the brain as part of the learning, so don't think I've lost my marbles along the way, it's designed that way for rapid learning.

I will also take the opportunity to thank you for purchasing this book and that you can and will pass the benefits of what you have gained from reading it to others.

I wish to thank my beautiful wife and mother who have been patient with me through this process.

We can all move towards making the world an even better place than it is today, even if we have to do it one person at a time, any journey begins with the first step.

Namaste

Darrell

What is Spirituality?

Everyone will have their own interpretation of its meaning; some may see it as I once did, as some form of religion. Personally I have not read one chapter of the bible, I don't need to nor do I have too.

To me Spirituality is all about discovering the Source energy from which we/everything emanate from and eventually, all be it at varying speeds, return too.

I will endeavour to help us discover the magnificence of it all as our minds open up to "*the truth*," something we already know deep within, as we also discover the reality of when working with our "*Source*", anything is possible.

Spirituality in its purest form, excludes no-one and no-thing, while religion may appear to segregate into groups, or cults/sects, Spirituality is a collective oneness.

To assist opening up our mind to our *Higher Self*, or as some would have it God, Jehovah, Allah, or Krishna, it really doesn't matter what we choose to call it, so long as we are aware of its existence, and that we are all a connected piece of it.

I will briefly explain that most of us predominately function from our five senses or our conscious mind, which isn't giving us a true picture of what we perceive, is going on within and around us.

Functioning predominately from our five senses, we generally think, move and respond to our immediate surroundings, usually missing the bigger picture totally and deal with the highs and lows, not really reaching our true potential/meaning.

I feel we need to function more in line with our subconscious mind and once we get this, life becomes truly phenomenal, life begins to flow, like a stream into a river and on into an ocean of abundance of all opportunities, a healthier, happier and a very rewarding lifestyle.

I don't expect everyone to take my word or at first believe everything in this book, in fact I would ask you to further your own research, gather the evidence as I have, this will help speed the process up.

We all have perceptions and I respect everyone to have them, science based facts and general life experience associations will assist to hasten our awakening or enlightenment.

All of what I am about to discuss is a mixture of personal experience, that most will co-relate with, backed by solid scientific evidence, evidence that can be readily and easily sourced with the help of today's technology.

The example I wish to give is with the title of this book "It Began With a Stubby" a stubby being a small glass/plastic fluid container mainly linked with alcoholic beverages, for this exercise I will use the glass example, it will help us learn just how much our conscious mind leaves out.

It will also assist in opening the mind to the sixth sense, and to the greater reality of what is really going on around us, so bear with me here and see how intriguing it becomes.

Truly, we are much, much more than what meets and greets the eye and most of us have grossly underestimated our real potential.

Sceptics

I am also aware there will be sceptics, I myself was once a total none believer, an atheist, a sceptic in the truest sense.

I am now becoming more totally contented with life in general realizing the truth.

Sceptics, doubters or others who simply don't wish to believe we are all a part of something massive, all linked in a mysterious way, may challenge the very essence of what I will be saying, and that's fine.

It is all a part of the learning by challenging our thoughts to go even deeper, we all attract and create our own thoughts and opinions about everything.

It Began with a Stubby, began for me in a local hotel/pub in the town I grew up in Mackie's Royal Hotel in Latrobe, Tasmania, Australia.

In a way it was just as confirmation for me as it was for the gentleman with whom I was stirring/explaining at the time, an awakening for both of us so to speak.

Also a display that the Divine energy, Source energy or again as some would have it God, doesn't expect us to take life or ourselves too seriously.

The discussion went like this.

I stated to the gentleman, having a pre-conceived idea as to what his response would be.

You're drinking a stubby!

How much did that cost you?" he replied, four bucks!

I playfully replied, four bucks!

Wow, how did you get it that cheap?

This then set the tone for the discussion, as he blurted out, cheap! Where the hell do you get cheap from?

Four bucks per bloody stubby isn't cheap!

This is how it went from there.

I explained the stubby is made of glass!

Where does that glass come from?

It comes from sand!

Ok, where does the sand come from?

Let's say at this point, from the beach, doesn't matter which beach or location at this time.

Sand, when intense heat *energy* is applied melts and when it cools, solidifies into glass.

Where does the beach come from?

With the oceans, pounding rock, crustaceans, shell fish, into fine particles and minerals, like a cake mix, the perfectly blended ingredient for glass, then depositing it upon our shores as sand.

The sand is transported to a foundry or blast furnace, and *energy*, heat, applied to it to be turned into glass.

How do we pick the sand up initially?

By loader or excavator then placed into a truck!

Where did the loader or excavator come from?

Being made of metal, the machinery and truck would obviously have been mined, processed, designed etc.; etc.

Where did the mine come from?

The metal processing plant, all buildings had to be designed then constructed; the mines obviously have machinery, explosives, planning personnel, fuels.

Everything that has transpired so far has all begun with the **thought** process.

Again bear with me, what we are ultimately endeavouring to achieve, is opening and enriching the **thought** processes, which will be of benefit as we move deeper into this book.

So far what we are establishing with all of these processes is the creation of thousands of jobs, mega millions of dollars having exchanged hands and we haven't yet loaded one grain of sand, and into what?

A truck, which essentially has moved through all the same or similar processes as the excavator/loader, they also have windows, more glass/sand.

The truck would have rubber compound tires which is an extract from tree's and also going through a manufacturing process.

The machinery and equipment have engines, and other components' which are manufactured in all countries around the world, this will now include aviation and shipping coming together to create the machinery, all well before the stubby has even been created.

Processes

The sand is then transported to the glass furnace which in turn encompasses more construction and planning.

The sand is then washed and refined before being turned into glass, all this machinery require fuels, oils and electricity for them to function, other sources of **energy,** which all have to be extracted from the earth.

Fuels and oils are transported by trucks and ships to and from all corners of the earth, and on and on it will go in an ever expanding never ending process.

The refinery which makes the glass requires **energy** to melt the sand, more equipment is required to form and make the stubby, form it into the shape it eventually becomes before it is then transported to the brewery to be filled with beer.

Who had the **thought, and where does a thought come from**? Who invented beer?

By now our minds would be beginning seeing a bigger picture and accepting there is more to it than initially meets the eye.

This process is important.

As we go deeper into the book as there is going to be some really challenging stuff for the mind to process, so while it may be a little strung out at the moment, what follows later won't be such a challenge.

Some by now may be saying, well they're mass produced, the reason for the cheaper price that our mind would be now processing.

Our conscious mind or **ego** mind will start giving us all sorts of messages and excuses by now but please, soldier on.

Similar processes apply to everything we purchase these days, but it's the process that's generally ignored.

A simple thing we just take for granted an everyday simple thing we can use and discard without given much or any **thought** at all as to its origin and what's involved.

Once we begin to look at the greater picture, life itself begins to take on a whole different meaning.

Once we're open to it, we then begin realizing that by living and working with the **source** of everything, we can have, become and basically do whatever we choose we want with life, be it health, wealth and abundance of all good things.

Anything we place **thoughts** of love upon, and we don't have a need to go to church unless we choose to, we are all a part of a greater magnificent **energy**, which will be explained in more detail in the following chapters.

Now back to the stubby process so we can finish off with it and move on.

Once the stubby reaches the brewery it is to be filled with a beverage, we'll say beer for now, which has had to be brewed with a combination of water, hops, malt, sugar and yeast.

All these ingredients have to be farmed, grown, harvested then transported from various areas and brought together to become beer.

It really doesn't matter what the contents of the stubby are, it could be apple cider involving apples, it could be wine involving grapes, what really matters is that all this is provided by mother nature.

Brewing

This is done in stainless steel vats, another product mined from the earth, as is all the other associated equipment within the beer making process.

All come from where?

A *thought/imagination!* And each of us has the capability to think and imagine.

The stubby also has a label on it which was once a part of a tree, again cut with chainsaws, transported and turned into wood chips, then turned into paper pulp, made into paper and then into the label which has a graphic design on it.

The stubby has a metal cap sealing it, mining involved again, it's placed in plastic wrap, a by-product of petro chemicals drawn from the earth by drilling oil wells.

Packed into cardboard cartons, more trees and processing ready for transportation to the hotel industry.

Some cartons of stubbies are usually stacked into refrigeration unites ready for the customer/consumer.

The bar person sells it to us for "FOUR BUCKS!" for goodness sake don't tell anyone, especially the government or up will go the taxes.

The whole process, from the beginning of nature through to the consumer, has along the way created directly and indirectly, hundreds of millions of jobs, billions of dollars have exchanged hands.

I say this in all sincerity as I have only scratched the surface of the true involvement.

If I were to continue to go into every minute detail I would be writing a whole book on this one example alone.

When I say scratched the surface, all the people involved have requirements as well such as the clothes, food, education, grooming ie; haircuts, dental work, homes to live in, transportation etc.

All of which require manufacturing of one form or another and on and on we could go in an endless quest never ever finding a true beginning or an end to it all.

My brother Peter once told me, well when we drink the stubby that's the end of it, and in a closed mind it is!

But it certainly isn't, as our bodies utilize the water and other ingredients to supply the cells of our bodies with *energy.*

We eliminate the toxins alcohol which is expelled via perspiration and urine which sometimes finds its way back to the ocean via the sewage systems, or excreted onto the ground where eventually the sun's rays would pick it up again.

With the natural process of evaporation and precipitation redeposit it back onto the earth somewhere in some place as rain.

Who knows? It may even end up back at the brewery!

Is spirituality religion?

At first I thought Spirituality was a form of religious practice, but as I've opened up to and discovered along the way Spirituality does not separate itself into groups, it is wholeness, a oneness.

So what does this stubby business have to do with *Spirituality* you may be beginning to wonder, it's really all about opening our minds to a bigger picture and done so using every day examples will help the process.

Everything begins with a *thought*, a notion; if it doesn't then we would never have evolved from being a cave man to where we are today!

Think about this for a moment.

Everything we have and experience today was all available to the caveman way back then.

All the cars/minerals were sitting in the ground waiting to be mined out, the fuel was there, the electrical energy was available, everything.

Therefore it is suffice to say, if everything was available to the caveman, and it was, then everything we need for the future must also be available to us right now also mustn't it?

We just need to tap into it with a necessity, a need, we will think about whatever it is we need and the answer will be provided.

So where does a **thought** come from?

Well our conscious mind would tell us, from our brain.

From my research, scientific studies now show us, if we move from auto pilot and tap into our subconscious or "God" conscious mind, the deeper level, the answers and solutions to every problem will materialize for us.

This doesn't work for a select few, but for each and every one of us.

Again what we are endeavouring to do with this book, is to help us come to the realization that we are all a part of something wonderfully massive.

This something, this energy, which flows through all of us flows through everything.

The same thing that beats all our hearts, that something that not only creates the oxygen we all breathe, also assists us to consume it without us having to consciously tell ourselves breathe in breathe out.

This one divine energy, or as some have it "God" consciences, works with us to survive.

It gives us all we need to strive and evolve effortlessly once we draw our attention to its existence and move from denial.

Accept it, flow with it, life then becomes not only effortless but fun as well.

I hope to help us realize there is much, much more to us than we may have to this point, ever begun to imagine.

It will sometimes be fun for most, may offend some and that will be because of our social conditioning, all of which I will endeavour to explain more clearly along the way.

Social conditioning

With the way we generally grow up and the level of success, Spirituality, criminality, depression, joy, happiness and abundance etc.; is all directly related and largely determined by the environment we are born into and brought up with.

This is not a time to blame our parents, siblings, peers, teachers etc.; they are only passing on the programming/conditioning from their parents, grandparents, and great grandparents!

There has never been a better time in history as to what we are learning now!

I began my path to *Spiritual* awakening moving through life on auto pilot generally bumping from perceived good luck to disaster and back again.

Being brought up by a self-confessed atheist my father, and social conditioning from extended family, peers and education facilities, so my awakening was slow in the beginning.

I had some religious backgrounding in the form of Sunday school during childhood, but to this day no formal religious training and personally none required.

I do realize that religion has served society for thousands of years and still has its place within society today for those who feel the comfort of group participation.

Personally, I am now finding the option of dealing directly with "head office" the better option, and again, this is my preference, I respect each and every one to the right of preference.

We are all born speaking one language

There is an amazing lady in Australia by the name of Barbra Dunstan, who after around eight years of researching discovered what in the beginning was an inkling, babies from zero to around twelve weeks of age have distinct sounding cries when requesting assistance.

There has been a lot of research in this area over hundreds if not thousands of years.

The Dunstan method truly hit home for me, and doing my research and experiments with it, I found her method spot on, very easy to understand and apply.

What evolved for me was the fact that every child born onto this planet for those first twelve weeks, all speak one language, just as Barbra Dunstan predicted.

All human babies, there are no exceptions, and the evidence of how I arrived at this conclusion is as follows.

Barbra Dunstan discovered that babies have a distinct cry, one for when its hungry, another for wind, another for tiredness, one for a dirty diaper etc.;

If we follow the chart she has developed and or review the DVD, it becomes very clear and distinct as to what the baby is telling us and we can respond accordingly and confidently to meet the needs of the child.

This immediately brings both child and parent a more contented start in life.

The Dunstan method can be likened to being in a supermarket or restaurant and eves dropping on others conversations, it becomes that clear.

From around twelve weeks onward, the child then becomes more aware and alert to its surroundings and as its senses develop.

Sight, sounds, smells, tastes and touches are beginning to develop along with the parental social conditioning.

Parents voice, handling and smell are all being established, some call it the bonding process.

I personally believe this begins within the womb, as baby feels every emotion its mother goes through as the body floods with endorphins during happiness, the adrenalin would also flow through bub if mum becomes fearful or excited.

We have already experienced babies suffering drug and alcohol withdrawal symptoms not long after birth as physical evidence that what mum consumes, so does bub.

We can take a child from birth, let's just say from China at this point, for no particular reason, just what entered my mind, raise it in Australia, Russia, America or London, and that child, although he/she will always look like its Chinese parents.

The child will now develop an Australian, Russian, American or prominent accent and the behavioural patterns of the step or fostering parents and cultural habits of that country as well through social conditioning.

We see it throughout the planet these days as multiculturalism spreads, so we don't really have to look far for the evidence.

The amazing fact being, in the instant we draw our first breath and for the first twelve weeks, we all speak a uniform, universal language and then lose it somewhere along the way.

Where did language begin to change?

Language is believed to have developed to the vibrational frequencies we call sound, happening around us.

Scientists believe that the vibrations and frequencies we pick up on is where language began to differentiate, we pick up the frequencies and decipher or turn them into sound.

The airwaves or frequencies vary from place to place, for an example the noises we hear from around the equator to those of the north and south poles would differ dramatically but still doesn't explain very clearly as to how our dialects were created, but they believe this is how we began to form words of communication.

I really struggle to come to terms with this as, if we look at the variation of the dialect of the English people, it varies from one end of London to the other and then we also have the Scottish and Irish dialect.

Throughout the Asian regions we have many variations also and to narrow it down if we take the Philippine's, there are supposedly eighty plus different dialect's as there are many Islands, but as they are grouped around the equator, one would think the noise exposure would be similar, but again it boils down to interpretation.

Small groups of people science indicates began to form their own interpretations or sounds from primal grunts into words and it spread out from there creating many and varied dialects.

In fact in the Philippines, the English language has become the second language as a way of communication.

The English language is now spreading globally, so much so, to the extent some languages are now disappearing as the generations pass. So will we as human beings eventually return to all speaking the one language as we do when we show up here?

Only time will tell and it would appear at this point in time that language would appear to be English.

Are we slowly evolving to the realisation that we are all one and not as separate as it would appear?

A point I am trying to get across, is that one of the great mentors of *Spirituality* going around today is, an amazing author and mentor Dr Wayne W Dyer puts it this way, "we are all a part of this great *UNI-VERSE, UNI* being *ONE* and *VERSE* being song, meaning the whole universe, including us, is all one song!

We are all a part of the one source, the one Divine energy, separate from no one or no-thing.

Example; be it a small one, but significant in its essence.

The tree requires carbons from the atmosphere for its survival.

We give off carbons when we breathe out, drive a car or whatever.

The trees ingest carbons and give off or exhale oxygen, which we cannot survive without.

Everything has its place whether we wish to believe it or not.

Everything has its place

Everything in this whole universe and for us predominately upon this amazing planet has such a delicate position removing one thing can upset the whole ecology.

At one time it was found viable to remove all the wolves from the Yukon in Canada; this would make it safer for tourists to camp in the area.

A few years later all the trees began unexplainably dying out, after years of head scratching and asking why? What's changed to have caused this to happen?

After not too much scientific study, someone stated, well we have only removed the wolves to make it safer for tourists to camp there, but what effect if any at all would the removal of the wolves have on why the trees are dying?

It was soon discovered that the removal of wolves to protect man while camping, had left the moose without any natural predators.

The moose population soon grew and grew, and as they renew their antlers each year, which has a velvet coating, they use the trees for rubbing it off.

The moose population became so large because their only natural predators were removed, the trees couldn't cope with all the animals rubbing the bark from them, ring barking kills the tree so when the question was asked, what has changed, and that would make this occur?

The answer was obviously the removal of one species, the wolf, with the reintroduction of the wolves, the Moose population soon returned to natural sustainable levels and the forests thrived once again, we can utilize everything in the environment if we approach it sensitively.

This one small example as to how sensitive and amazing this whole universal is and how source energy functions, and as to how we/everything are linked.

All the challenges we seem to encounter only serve as lessons, it would seem that we serve our time on planet earth as a form of schooling. We make mistakes, learn from them and make a record of it... What for? I often wonder.

False social conditioning

False social conditioning according to quantum physicists is called meme's or meme-tics pronounced meemes.

Meme's are not reality or truths as we would call it, an example of this would be the white lines or markings/signage on our roadways.

Rules are made up by governments and we generally follow them on auto pilot.

We are fear base trained and conditioned not to cross the white lines so we see them as a barrier or perceive them as such.

We won't cross them, generally for a fear of being punished by a hit in the wallet, monetary fine or the removal of our license, the privilege to drive.

A thing similar applies with signage, if we see a sign that has a 50 painted on it, we slow down unconsciously because we are conditioned, trained or programmed to do so in the belief that it will save someone's life.

In reality if we step out in front of a truck doing 10klms per-hour could kill us.

The road toll continually fluctuates generally in an upward trend, so until we build accident proof people and vehicles, it really won't matter how many signs and how much paint we apply to our roads.

The point is we are socially conditioned to conform as the governments continue introducing new "MEMES" rules and or laws for us to be conditioned too.

I am not saying for a moment that we should all rush out and flaunt the law, but rather helping us to awaken to the reality that as conditioned beings it can be difficult to see the bigger picture.

Beginning to see the bigger picture and what I am eluding too.

What we place our attention upon we bring into reality, once we begin truly embracing and understanding **spirituality** or as some may call it **law of attraction.**

What is the Law of Attraction?

Source energy or *God*, or for that matter *Allah*, call it Fred it doosn't mind what you call It, It lovingly gives to us what we place our attention upon in such a loving endless amount and abundance be it good thoughts or bad.

Now we really should be becoming more aware of exactly what we are thinking about, what media we consume etc., etc.

There are no exceptions to the abundance of what we consciously feed into our subconscious, what we think about we bring about period!

So before we begin saying I think Darrell is losing his marbles, or going loopy, can I say this.

When Christopher Columbus had a notion that the world was round, the masses laughed and ridiculed him, even gave him the oldest boat in the fleet initially to drop off the edge of the world.

Of cause we now know how silly that is today and of course the quality of ship he was given improved once his brilliance became apparent.

What the masses thought at the time was for them a truth, the world was actually flat, and that was only around 500 years or so ago.

Not that long ago if we take into context that human being has inhabited the planet for a few million years.

Benjamin Franklin, another loopy character who once had this silly notion that the world/universe was **energy** and if we could harness this **energy**, we could have something we label electricity.

He stood out in electrical storms flying a kite with a key metallic object attached to the string line attached to his kite.

Again the masses labelled him as someone rather eccentric.

We now build our cars, homes, aircraft, cook our food, communicate with one another, do virtually everything and complain even when we lose the power, thank God for this originally eccentric labelled gentleman.

One for thinking outside the square and two for not falling to the ridicule of the masses as neither will I.

Note;

One more interesting note here is, is it was also believed a lightning strike hitting the sand as to how glass was first discovered.

We can go on and on with the discussion of eccentric people.

We had Thomas Edison, who discovered/created the light bulb; he failed over one thousand times in his quest to create his light bulb, and was continuously asked/told to give it up.

His persistence gave birth to his dream that of which we mostly just take for granted today and thank god for him for taking his time to *think outside the square and persist* even when he was continually told to give up.

I don't place myself in the same category as these great geniuses of their time, only to be as persistent in my quest to help people, realize the genius within.

The God consciousness which flowed through those people then, we today now recognize as geniuses of their time.

They each were labelled as eccentric in their time.

This same intelligent energy they consciously connected with, also continues to flow through us right in this moment as it did back then and has done so for billions of years as quantum physicists are now telling us.

Again I don't mind what at all what label anyone chooses, I respect everyone to have their own opinions and what anyone says or thinks about me isn't any of my business.

Therefore am unaffected by it, my sole and main purpose again, is to help others open up their minds to the fact that once we align ourselves with our **source energy**, we can all achieve any and everything we can put our minds upon.

Create a better healthy less stressful life for the whole of humanity and the world we live in.

A great affirmation of Dr Wayne W Dyer's

Keep in mind the ancient simple truth that, "the mighty oak was once a little nut that held its ground." You are a mighty oak in the making, and it's alright to be a little nutty as long as you also hold your ground!

A few more examples;

Now back to the examples, with the rising road toll for instance.

With ever increasing technology, improving our roads, imposing speed limits introducing new road rules, the cars are built with more and more safety features on a daily basis.

Why then do our road tolls continue to increase, frustrating the police and law makers and breaking the hearts of families far and wide?

Given that we are learning, what we place our attention upon becomes our reality, and with all the endless media coverage, television, newspapers, the internet, twitter, discussing it with family friends, peers etc. filling our focus with every macabre detail over and over, we subconsciously feel the emotions, the grief for the families, the rage at yet another speedster, drunken or inattentive driver needlessly taking lives!

It would appear to be an outlandish statement or notion to say that during these moments we could be attracting very similar circumstances into our lives.

I have gathered vast amounts of evidence of so called coincidences where family members have been devastated and grieved, only to suffer similar circumstances a short time (days, weeks or only a few months later) and saying "how could God be so cruel to us?"

But as we go further into how and why these things happen, briefly, our subconscious or God conscious mind cannot see what it is we want and acts entirely upon the information we feed into it.

It thinks every emotion or powerful emotion is what we are asking for and moves people events and circumstances to ensure that what we are feeling most strongly about is actually what we want.

And when we get more of what we want or don't want, how many times we have heard the statement God he/she has all the luck! or gee that poor bugger is having a run of bad luck! Or luck (good or bad) just seems to follow them around!

And it could be said then, why doesn't it happen in mass proportions?

Well it does, and again we see the evidence of it everywhere, with floods, earth quakes and tsunamis, and we don't link these things to the media with this because it doesn't have to be the exact circumstance every time.

More recently we saw evidence of a couple who just escaped the rail tunnel bombings in England.

A few years later got caught up in the devastating floods in Queensland Australia, and a few weeks after that, just happened to be in Christchurch in New Zealand during their massive earthquake.

They seemingly kept on moving into the path of devastation and never understanding why, but kept reliving each encounter via the media and whoever else was prepared to listen.

We also don't link some of our circumstances to the movies we watch, when our fears and emotions are interfered with something chronic.

We attract love when we watch and feel loving movies, we attract fear when we watch horror movies, and there is so much information for us to digest.

We see someone who wins the lotto, and think oh the lucky buggers, why couldn't it be me?

Instantly feeling a lack of money and wonder why we attract lack to ourselves, instead of feeling the joy for them and imagining what it would be feeling like to be in their position, then attracting similar circumstances to ourselves.

I would at this time encourage you to put the book down for a little while and digest the past couple of paragraphs and try to relate any similar circumstance you may have encountered in your lifetime, and if your only young, question some older family members about any coincidences they may have experienced.

Because what we are trying to develop with this book is to have a continual awakening or opening up to the sixth sense which is the narrator of our lives more so than our five senses which do not give us a true reflection of life as it should be.

Bear in mind that I myself being brought up as an *atheist* was massively sceptical and it has taken me many years to open up to it and today am still opening up and learning as I go along.

I just want to share how it has happened for me, as it will happen differently for each and every one of us.

My journey has had many and varied authors and teachers whose teachings have opened up a little bit at a time and has now culminated for me and into this book of which you are holding and reading because you were meant too, the same way as I am driven to write it.

Learning spirituality, like learning to play sport, or become very proficient at our job, even writing a book, it is and always will be an ongoing process, the more we apply ourselves to it, the more **the law of attraction** will support us, and the better we become.

Everything in life is a continuum of evolution, if it were not; we would still be sitting in caves, wondering where our next meal was coming from.

I say without conviction that we really need to retrain how we think, beginning at the primary school level and even before.

As I stated earlier, there is now concrete scientific evidence that from conception to the birth, we experience every emotion mother does, so are therefore being programmed prior to birth.

Some children are born alcoholics or having withdrawal symptoms from illicit drug's so new mums find it difficult to cope with their newborns, so we label them as mentally unstable, manic depressive and a host of other things that comes to mind, top them up with prescription drugs and put them on suicide watch for post natal depression.

We only have to look no further than our native relatives in remote areas free of drugs, alcohol and other negative behaviours to see that none of these things exist.

We as a society create them, and have Doctors who mean well giving us all these reasons as to why we need to put our new mums on some kind of anti-depressant, further compounding the problem and actually creating a greater challenge in society without even realizing that they are unconsciously being the educated part of the root cause.

Our subconscious can and will be trained to do anything

Human beings can be trained to do anything, smoking cigarettes is a classic example.

In the beginning we were bombarded with big strong good looking people, actors and actresses smoking (even doctors) so, it must be good for us.

It became so ingrained in society that today governments struggle convincing people it isn't good for them and at the same time, pouring billions of public dollars into advertising against a habit it made legal and now trying to reverse.

In fact where once we shared cigarette's around freely, people have now reverted to stealing them, robbing people to feed a habit that we have subconsciously created ourselves by using unconsciously the *law of attraction*.

We have created what was once sociable and fashionable, now into criminals and devastating health challenges for millions of people.

Once we wake up how to utilise the *law of attraction*, we can really turn any perceived problems around.

When we come to the realization and accept that we all breathe the same air, share the same water, recycling everything including our bodies and we all share the same universal *energy*.

The same *energy* beating not only my heart, your heart, but that of every living and perceived non living creature, vehicle, dwelling, everything within the whole universe is created with this never ending cycle of *energy*, excluding no one and no-thing, there are no exceptions.

When we begin to move beyond the concept of our five senses, where science estimates our conscious mind processes around seven to eleven bits of information per second, our subconscious mind is estimated to be able to process around ten trillion bits of information per second.

If we take snapshots look at that.

We can understand that our heartbeats happen unconsciously, our lungs inhale and exhale unconsciously, the female builds and eliminates the reproductive eggs without conscious *thought*, infact some will consciously complain as this happens.

We break our skin or bones and repair ourselves unconsciously, process the air we breathe so as every one of our estimated one hundred trillion cells are oxygenated simultaneously.

The mind boggles if we were to try and do all these things consciously we wouldn't get anything done.

It's also estimated that everyone develops at least four types of cancer during a lifetime and eliminates it without us even being consciously aware of it.

It is also estimated that we use around one third of our brain capacity in our lifetime and that would be right as each of us use only around a third of what our computers are capable of before we purchase another one!

A waste really isn't it?

When we are capable of achieving so much more, and the beauty of this we don't have to go away and study to become a Rhodes Scholar or become some kind of decorated academic to tap into what we are truly capable of.

Personally I never achieved the required passes to get into an apprenticeship I thought I would have loved to create a career.

I was told that I would struggle in school and I proved my detractors 100% correct by reaching my potential of a 100% academic failure.

Being told I was going to be a failure and believing the academically trained mentors, how could I not achieve what I was told?

I was a day dreamer but I achieved everything I was told I was going to achieve, simply because I listened socially conditioned and responded accordingly; I attracted the tertiary results I and everyone else expected!

Am I seeking sympathy for that?

No way.

I worked diligently within the construction and mining industry where my skills operating heavy machinery were soon recognized so much so that I became trained to teach others my skills.

Soon with my personal interaction skills with people and encouragement from my mentors, my ability to teach and nurture others within the mining industry encouraging others to become the best and most proficient they could become, has lead me to the profession I am currently in as I write this book, a skills teacher.

The success I have as a teacher, has past students to this day still keep in contact with me mainly because they tell me I gave them the inspiration to go for anything and are all achieving in their own right.

This is my reward today, so no, no sympathy required, and via this book, if I can achieve helping *one* person become aware of how we can be, do and have whatever we want, then it will be a success.

As we delve further into our spirituality and develop a greater understanding of how *source energy* works for us, and it is giving 24hours a day 365days a year (366 on leap years) and not as most religions would have us believe, five or six days a week, some arguing that God or Allah's day of rest is either on a Saturday or a Sunday.

Incidentally if this were to happen we couldn't exist, I mean, who would beat our hearts for us?

All the animals would drop, the world would stop revolving at dizzying speeds and mother earth would stop hurtling through space at thousands of miles/kilometres an hour and have to be parked up!

Seriously, I am not trying to denounce religion as such, more to the point I am trying to state fact. Our loving energy source doesn't just work for some and not for others.

When it shuts us down on one side of the world, (with the exception of continuous shift workers) while we rest, repair and regenerate ourselves, it has the other half of the world arising and running around working to sustain the rest of us.

While still continuing to keep most of us alive as we sleep, bringing into the world new born while removing others who have served their time, forever recreating itself through us.

It's ironic that as most religions also teach us that on God or whoever's day of rest must be pestered with having to listen to us confess our sins.

In actual fact all we need to do is give total forgiveness and I don't mean half-heartedly, to ourselves and those with whom we may have offended or hurt in any way shape or form.

If we do this in all sincerity, heartfelt and honestly, forgiveness is instantaneous, without question.

This doesn't mean confessing rushing out and killing fellow man and confessing or asking forgiveness, thinking all will be well, as the rule, *do unto others as you would have them do unto you* definitely applies.

The more love we give, the more love comes back, the more hatred we give, the more comes back to us, *its law*, even though it may not happen instantly, it will and does happen without fail.

The latest evidence we have of this *do unto others* has been demonstrated in Australia with the underworld street wars where the "underbelly" has all but virtually wiped itself out, purely with hatred taking care of hatred.

You see, if we to harm someone, consciously we expect to be caught or have someone seek revenge on behalf of the/ our victim, it's impossible at a subconscious level for people in those circumstances, not fear/think retribution for their actions and in doing so receive it.

It could be argued, what about those unsolved murders/ kidnappings?

Again sometimes their hand of fate maybe a car accident, or because of the subconscious stress or remorse, they virtually eat themselves up from the inside with cancers or strokes, heart disease, how many times do we hear of bedside confessions just before a perpetrators death?

A confession, and invariably they speak of the miserable lives they have had to live because of what they've done. But I am neither going to be judge nor jury, I just need to be the best I can be.

So what is energy, what does it look like?

Who knows? Again what I've learned from my limited religious training is that it is some dead white spirit floating around in a place called heaven!

But my perception has changed dramatically since then.

As we know energy is an ever changing vibration, from one form to another never remaining still.

The wind is energy, lightening is energy, it (lightening) creates nitrogen and is delivered to the earth via the rain as food for plant life, we can assist in creating energy with water moving through turbines to create electricity.

The sun, is energy, the fuel we put into our cars is a form of energy and when burned changes as it returns back into the atmosphere as Co'2's to also become food for the trees which we have discussed previously this is putting it into a simple perspective.

We have so much other energy as well; we can dig up uranium which is another form of energy, we use energy to extract it, something we are still learning about (trial and error) and that's how we evolve.

Every accident or incident we instinctively investigate so as not to repeat the same mistakes, so are there accidents? Or are they lessons to help us evolve for a better future?

There are many self-help books now out there, and once our mind is open to it, we attract them into our life or they will attract us.

You will find what I am saying isn't just something I've dreamt up, the sayings *seek and ye shall find* and *ask and it will be given* will become more relevant to us as we see the *law of attraction* working for us.

How many universal
laws are there?

So is there more than the *law of attraction* involved in this?

Yes there is.

We understand that Isaac Newton discovered the *law of gravity*, there is also the **law of giving**, the **law of receiving**, the **law of forgiveness**, the **law of gratitude** and of cause the **law of attraction** itself, the **law of increase**, and the **law of thinking**, also the **law of supply**, the **law of compensation**, the **law of obedience**, as well as the **law of sacrifice**, to name the important ones to place ourselves on the path to success.

Most teachers or avatars' of spirituality usually skirt around the use of the word God because a lot of teachings or significant numbers of them are involved in various religions and have tarnished the name of God by abusing their positions by taking advantage of others.

So much to the extent as soon as it's mentioned unfortunately, many people turn away from learning more of how it works for us and always giving in an unconditional loving manner.

Again as strangely as it may seem, because along with you the reader, I too have received things that I could have sworn I have never asked for.

In the beginning, this is the difficult thing to understand and come to terms with, again, bear with me and maybe I can help throw some light onto it as we get further in.

It may appear that I am giving religion a bit of a bashing, but not at all, I do care about everyone and everything and religion has and is serving humanity as we have been awakening to our true spirituality.

So please forgive me if it appears this way, in all honesty I am not knocking religion or encouraging anyone to walk away from it as it has and is serving to keep the message alive, we are just progressing now.

Making direct communication with our source, freeing up the middle man to follow other pursuits if they so choose to do so, or broaden their own personal knowledge in helping others find their way.

Some of the greatest teachers to have ever graced this planet, were not Christians, Muslims or Buddhists and or whatever.

Jesus Christ wasn't a Christian, indications are he studied Hindu, but he knew how to make direct contact with the ever loving invisible force, something Jesus tried to teach us we are all capable of, and so Christianity was built off of him!

Similarly, Gautama Buddha wasn't a Buddhist, Buddhism was built off of him as a teacher, these people were great metaphysicians, so switched on as to how to be at peace, help heal and bring love to all and those who chose to be close to them.

We have people today who are very well up there as well, the recently expired Maharishi Mahesh Yogi, the founder of Transcendental Meditation who also spiritually mentored the famous sixties pop group the Beatles, was very in tune with our higher self.

Mother Theresa being another and the Dali Lama is another very high spiritual avatar who amazingly, has no home, no bank account, so no bills to pay etc.; no stress to speak of, but because of his connection, he is so cared for, and loved by millions across the world.

The Dali Lama travels to all corners of the earth, that's a figure of speech; there are no corners on a round planet! Meeting with the who's who in all perceived powerful places.

Get it? no job, no home, no bank account, no global financial crisis, yet is privy to travel at will, stay in all the best places if he so chooses to do so, all because he trusts and has the faith to be looked after by a greater power than any government may think it has.

Governments come and go with the blink of an eye the Dali Lama serves humanity, unconditionally sending expressions of love and care even for his detractors.

Considered one of the most influential governments on the planet today, the Chinese government which controls most of the planets wealth, has no power whatsoever over breaking the spirit of the Dali Lama, it has tried for years without a hint of success, such is the personal power has the Dali Lama by remaining connected to our source!

Like the honey bee to the flower

How does the Law of Attraction work?" The law of attraction, as stated earlier, whether we wish to believe it or not, it is working for/with us continuously, 100% of the time twenty four seven, three sixty five (366) every leap year all of our lives!

This may be hard to come to terms with because we have things happen in our lives that we are totally sure we have never asked for, and don't worry I will share things with you as we proceed of some of the perceived hardships (bad luck) I've encountered along the way to show you that you are not alone.

The fact is that I did, and coming to this realization of the *law of attraction*, begin working with it helped turn my life around, as it will everyone if who so chooses to embrace the reality (truth) of it and faith in it.

What I have discovered with the help of science and many teachers is that the whole universe is a vibrational energy vibrating at varying speeds and frequencies.

Everything we perceive as solid matter is all constructed by molecules, atoms and particles that reduce down in size that even with today's technology cannot measure it so minute are these particles we only know of their existence by the evidence they leave behind, like forensic investigations picking up the invisible trail criminals leave behind.

Other examples I give may seem ludicrous or way out there, again scientifically proven, but I will endeavour to explain it in enough detail to help us understand so we don't need to go on a bewildering fact finding search.

Let's begin with a big one.

Quantum physicists are now telling us that the whole universe is totally silent!

That's right, you are reading right, "silent," there is simply no sound.

All sound or noise we create within our own minds/brain.

Our perception of noise or sound is a varying vibration that we pick up with our outer ears and via a series of functions, like the inner ear drum transferring the vibration to a nerve ending creating an electric impulse transferring the message into the brain for processing it into sound or noise.

A simple example would be, if a deaf person is reading this, they would be nodding knowingly as when we don't have these functions we take for granted as normal, it gives more meaning.

We have a voice box which has vocal cords much like the strings of a guitar, which vibrate as we send the air we breathe through them with fluctuating force and our tongue and mouth form the words we struggled to learn as a child and use fluently today.

We send the vibration out to the receiver who then deciphers the vibrations as words, grunts whistling etc., and it depends upon the focus of the receiver as to what we say or sing as to whether they get the information correctly, as there are many vibrations being picked up simultaneously, back ground vibrations like radios, television, traffic, weather etc. that the brain has to process all at the same time.

To further explain this, if we were standing face to face chatting directly, it would appear that there were sounds being emanating from my mouth, but if I were to call you from another country on the phone or over the internet via

Skype, would it be my voice you were hearing over hundreds or thousands of kilometres/miles?

Or is it a vibration being transmitted via satellite to the speakers of your phone or computer?

This happens right across the planet/universe, amidst trillions of other vibrations and frequencies. Just give that a little thought for a while and digest it if you must.

It's probably a good time to put the book down and have a think about it so our brain doesn't fry.

If we are watching the news or sports on television, is it the news reader or sports commentator you are hearing?

Who incidentally are being transmitted virtually globally simultaneously, or is it a vibration from your speakers being transferred across the room to you?

Our five senses would be telling us that this is just sound, but you can turn the telly off, or hit the mute button on the remote control, and its silent to us at least, and we can step outside and still experience the silence.

Because, unless we tune into it with some hand held device virtually anywhere, it's there, we just are not able to consciously tune into it using our five senses.

At this point you may be beginning to question what I am saying within your own mind, something we all really know, but have doubted because of our social conditioning that the whole universe could be a vibration and not physically solid as it appears to be.

Sight is another vibration, when we video ourselves playing in the snow or on a beach somewhere and we go home and watch it on the telly or on the camera playback function, is it really us we are watching or a vibrational image made up of rapidly moving pixels?

Similarly if we video a blind person moving around and again we wish to watch the replay, we see it, but the blind person, because of sensory malfunction, be it in the receiver, the eyes or the transmitter signal to the brain via a neurotransmitter, the image we see of the blind person, simply does not exist for them.

We watch the Olympics, any sport for that matter on the screen in our lounge room, being transmitted from anywhere on the planet, supposedly as it happens live, all this is being transmitted into homes and venues to every part of the planet.

Again we can again walk outside and look around, do we see the sports taking place?

They are there, happening, as are the emails, text messages, radio waves, news broad casts etc., are all happening, but as we are not personally tuned into it, we have no awareness of it.

Our conscious mind, which functions only on what our five senses are focused upon and nothing much else misses so much that is actually going on around us.

What I am trying to establish here for us is how the *law of attraction* works, is in a fairly complex way of vibrations and frequencies.

Once our minds can begin to accept this concept of what is truly going on in and around us, when we tune into whatever it is we want as we think in pictures and images.

When we get highly emotional feeling really excited about anything, think as though we already have it, it is really ours, people events and circumstances bring it into our reality.

Again it does this 24/7, whether we are thinking good thoughts or bad, it really doesn't matter, it will give us more of the similar circumstances of what our main attention is upon, and does so always lovingly and unconditionally.

Events, people and circumstances happen; molecules and particles which are the essence of everything in the universe including us and referred to as photons are magically and magnetically drawn together into the manifestation of creation.

Once we understand this we will become more conscious of what we are going to be thinking about so we are bringing into creation not only a better world for us all to live in, but a much better life is created for us individually.

Although we are all a part of one collective consciousness and therefore should treat each other with the same respect we treat and expect for ourselves.

I could go on and on about the area of vibrations and frequencies, but in general we have the concept already.

Sensory malfunctions

It's common knowledge now that we have our five senses, and there are people all around us who have sensory malfunctions, i.e., blindness, so no sense of sight, others have no sense of smell, deafness is obviously a hearing sensory malfunction, and we also have people with pain sensory malfunctions.

Therefore we can ascertain now that everything functions from the brain, and, during our lifetime scientists estimate we use only one third of it.

Sadly with social conditioning and governing by the law makers, we are retarded and restricted from reaching our true potential.

Thankfully people are waking up to this and the negative naysayer's will unfortunately be left behind a little at first until they let their ego's go and open up to the truth.

Instead of labelling people with sensory malfunctions these days as different, we are now assisting to function as what we regard as normal and learning new things along the way.

One such example is a young American soldier who lost both eyes, the windows to the brain/soul in Afghanistan.

By applying the vibration/frequency principle, a scientist has now developed a receptor, implanting it to his tongue for a trial basis and connecting it to his nervous system, ultimately with his optical sensory.

This young man can pick up the vibrations of his surroundings and transfer them into images within his mind, thus seeing what we see with our eyes via an implant within his tongue, similar to that of a mobile phone camera.

Truly amazing, and bearing this in mind, the ability to tap into this technology has been around since the cave man roamed the earth, we just hadn't evolved enough at that time in history.

We also see examples of where people learn to manage without arms, feeding, driving themselves around in automobiles adapted for them, let us able bodied persons even contemplate feeding ourselves with our feet?

Yet it can be done, or drive a car, wipe our bottoms for that matter, and with the last scenario we have developed a bidet toilet system that can wash and dry our bottoms for us today.

If we think about it, this opportunity has been available forever; only when one becomes tired of struggling out of necessity do we **ask the question**, what can we do to change this?

It then comes into play *ask and ye shall receive*, the answer to any challenge will come to mind, our job only is to act upon the answer provided.

Where do thoughts come from?

When we ask the question only then will an answer come to us, and from where?

Our conditioning will tell us from our brain and from nowhere else, but when we realise our sixth sense comes into play and we tap into our source and trust it unwaveringly, can we resolve any circumstance, create and bring into creation anything, anything at all if we so desire.

So where does the thought come from?

It comes from the same place the television signals come from, the radio waves, text messages and emails come from, again because we mainly choose to function from our five senses we are oblivious to the reality of it.

Even when we are using it on a daily basis we generally run along on auto pilot, taking whatever life deals up to us, wondering why some have all the luck and others appear to struggle through life's journey.

There are many who now understand and function from their unconscious/subconscious mind and the numbers are increasing at a phenomenal rate thanks to the efforts of a lady by the name of Rhonda Byrne who brought together some of the greatest teachers who live and teach this stuff daily.

Rhonda Byrne created a film/DVD called *THE SECRET* which has gone viral around the globe faster than any other movie I know, it had some governments banning it, I guess through a fear of people being able to think for themselves rendering them obsolete as governments require the dependence of the masses to feed their ego's need to control.

While this may not happen overnight, it is happening as I am writing this, people are being sick and tired of being begged to vote only to be told how they must live and obey our so called self-appointed leaders; people are becoming smarter in general.

The movie THE SECRET only scratched the surface of how it works, but millions of people myself included could relate to it, and of cause, like this book, everyone else is now spreading their perception of how it all works.

As with this book, it will resonate with some and not with others, but hopefully give every reader some extra insight into how The Law of Attraction works and make life and the world an even more beautiful positive place to live than it already is.

As one of the great spiritual teachers of today Dr Deepak Chopra explained while learning from one of his mentors Maharishi Yogi as they were preparing to build his (Maharishi's) spiritual centre.

One of the group asked, where is all the money going to come from to build this?

Without so much as a questioning thought, Maharishi replied, from where ever it is at the moment!

His reply was instantaneous, no lingering doubt, he knew without any fear the term ASK AND IT IS GIVEN or ASK AND YE SHALL RECEIVE.

These people make conscious contact with the infinite source or the Law of Attraction and work with it 24/7 they know how it works, not just for them, but for every one of us.

The Law of Attraction is a universal law, as is the law of gravity, the laws are not something created by man in that exceed

110Klms per hour (in Australia) and you will be fined and or lose demerit points from a drivers licence.

These are universal laws that have been around since the beginning of time.

Unlike the man-made laws they cannot be repealed, ignored or changed in anyway, to think otherwise would be foolish, and it isn't just designed for Australians, Americans and the Chinese, it's the absolute same for each and every one of us.

Emotions play an important role

As we move on and learn more about ourselves, "we are much greater than our five senses and conscious mind would have us believe" again you will know all this, all I am going to do is hopefully give it some more meaning, put it into a different perspective as to how it all ties in.

We have many and varied emotions such as anger, happiness, sadness, bliss, joy and depression, all of which have varying levels of intensity depending upon the circumstances.

For example, we can be sad because our sporting team lost, which may not have the intensity or power associated with the loss of a loved one, similarly, we can be happy to win ten dollars, but the intensity of that compared to winning ten million dollars may not be comparable, but they are examples of sadness and happiness at varying levels.

We can have tears of sadness and tears of joy, tears of pain or loss, we can move from one emotion to another within the beat of the heart or the blink of an eye.

An example of this would be while watching a favourite sports person (it may be a family member) leading the pack going for gold.

We can be euphoric as they approach the finish line in an unbeatable position, jumping up and down screaming our lungs out hugging those closest to us as we know how hard the athlete has worked and deserves this moment of glory, feeling the adrenaline rush and our hearts beating at an enormous rate, and then...

Oh no, they stumble and break down two meters from the finish, their career over in the blink of an eye as the other contestants run past, this how quickly things can change if we choose to get caught up in the moment, how long we linger in the moment of despair and heartbreak is again entirely up to us.

Why do **we allow** ourselves to feel these emotions?

Especially if we aren't even participating, only spectating.

Well it comes back to our conditioning, we see it all the time in everyday life, in every sport we choose to watch, or dancing competitions, even passive feel good reality TV shows **we choose** to watch and allow it to affect us emotionally.

It's simply **our choice** to watch it and our choice as to how we allow it affects us.

We can switch off any time we want, as no-one forces us to watch anything, we voluntarily participate in allowing our emotions to be in a conscious state and find it difficult to detach ourselves.

We are unconsciously attracting the sad or angry circumstances to ourselves but we generally don't associate it.

It doesn't happen instantly either, or are they the exact same circumstances, so we just fob it off as either good or bad luck and think nothing more of it.

Actually it was more recently discovered by some of those in the know, that subliminal messages were include in advertising and even movies.

If you are not familiar with subliminal messages, they are one line messages (affirmations) that can be included in movies, mainly in advertising as they are or were more readily flashed on the TV and consciously we thought we weren't taking any notice of it.

These messages would be flickering at such a fast speed we couldn't detect it with the naked eye, but the subconscious mind could see and read it clearly.

This method (now illegal and supposedly scrutinised by the security watch dog) would have us going out and purchasing things we didn't even want or need, such is the power of subliminal conditioning, playing with our emotions and they do it with our curious consent.

Here is another example.

How many of us say "these things happen in threes?"

I remember my parents telling me, "things usually happen in threes!" and if our parents tell us something especially when we're young and impressionable it must be true, well mustn't it?

And of cause then that statement was supported by others, so before long it was set in concrete, ingrained into the subconscious mind, and as regular as clockwork it happened.

If I had a puncture, I knew I could expect more, and sure enough, a week or a month later I would have had another two!

Can you relate to this?

When someone I knew died, I would scan the death notices until I found another two people I knew, it may have taken a week or two but it would surely happen, just so I could justify my conditioned mind that it happened in three's.

It wouldn't matter if I saw five people I knew had crossed over (passed away) I wouldn't mind the other two as I had justified in my mind with the first three and that's all that mattered.

Just like poker machine addiction, no different, even if they win a hundred thousand dollar jackpot, they will almost as surely put it all back through in an endeavour to have another win, just to feel that winning feeling again.

Even though they know the odds are stacked against them, their subconscious mind is programed to lose it all, in fact they expect it, as they see it on TV they read about their chances of losing it all, so they do.

How many times do we repeatedly see road carnage plastered through the media, and then a short time later, see more of the same.

Sometimes we see families suffer multiple tragedies, only weeks or a month or two apart?

We see it time and time again, but again brush it off as simply bad luck.

The more powerful our emotions, the more likely we are to attract it to us, and the more powerful we feel the emotion, the faster we are likely to attract it.

Again I stress that we can change our thoughts and emotions within the blink of an eye or in a heartbeat, so we have the power to change what we attract at any given moment once we are aware of what's really happening so as not to dwell in gloom and doom irrespective of what is currently going on around us.

Another interesting note mentioned recently, we had the Royal wedding, one female commentator said it will be interesting to watch the spike in births in the 36 weeks following the Royal wedding.

As the world looked on and felt the love and romance of the moment, the effect it has on some is amazing.

It's true, just do the research and look at the stats.

Although personally I am not big on statistics, they are just numbers like people dying in "threes" it is said statistics have a one in ten failure rate and even that statistic isn't right!

But it will be interesting to watch the birth spike following the royal wedding just the same out of curiosity.

We are one with water

The human body as science has proven and tell us, we are 75% water our brain is around 83%.

It's the water right now that I wish to focus upon at this point to help us to discover more as to how it functions and responds to our emotions, and at the same time further enhance our spiritual awakening, our spiritual connection to one another.

The proof

If we take the stubby metaphor and apply it to the water factor, we will begin to see what I am saying about every droplet of water.

The water that nourishes our bodies, our planet, everything, has been recycled through every being, every plant and animal. Not only has it passed through everyone and everything since the beginning of time, it will continue to pass through not only us, but everything else for eons to come.

This has to be, an unwritten law, to survive as a species, as a planet, as a universe, this must and will continue to happen, as I've stated we would cease to exist if it were not to be!

This may become a little nauseating for some or a little graphic so I will apologise for it now and will lead into it as gently as possible so it is easier to accept.

Let's, start with a tree.

Trees attract water, the more trees of course the more moisture they attract, hence the term (rain forest) the trees attract it naturally with a minimum of fuss as they require it, they are in harmony with nature.

We see hard evidence of this when we clear fell forests and replace them with farms, as the areas (farming land) disrupts the cycle, we turn to irrigation to grow grass and crops, we divert streams, build dams etc. then wonder why the whole eco system suffers.

I am not saying we can't utilise the forests to build our homes and paper industries, as Mother Nature will always bat last and eventually restore nature to her glorious best.

I am saying we can live and work the forests in harmonious ways for centuries to come if we are smart about how we choose to deal with it by replacing what we remove.

As a tree ends its growth cycle and seemingly dies, we see it drying out, where does this moisture go?

Obviously the sun's rays penetrate the very core of the tree (as it does to the core of the earth) and draws the moisture back into the atmosphere, and as we are aware, the evaporation cycle is taking place and eventually the tree dries out we then generally utilise it for other things like fire wood, furniture, paper and whatever.

We don't place any attention as to where the evaporated water has gone, but let's say it goes into the atmosphere as it does.

Then of course as it cools off we have the precipitation effect, cloud build up, turns into rain and returns to the earth either into a stream, into water tanks etc., to once again nourish the earth in one way or another.

We even run water through a power generator system to create power (energy) to warm our homes or give us light. All this is provided to us at no cost whatsoever (governments and electricity suppliers may charge us but our source supplies it free.

Moving on from the tree, what about animals?

Where does the moisture from their bodies go?

If we are observant enough, we will see the carcass virtually drying out before our eyes.

Some would appear to return into the earth as nutrients to feed the plants and of course again the sun's rays would draw it back into the atmosphere for the evaporation, precipitation cycle to take place.

Eventually it will return to earth, nourishing all living creatures which would exclude no-one and no-thing.

Are we beginning to form the picture within in our minds now that we are all apart of each other and everything?

Everything, including us (our bodies at least) is being recycled, and bear in mind all this has been happening since the beginning of time.

Just to emphasize this point a little further and probably not to everybody's taste, we see animal droppings, such as dog, cow and horse droppings in various stages of drying out and we don't really now have to question as to where the moisture goes.

The rest of it breaks down and is served as nutrients in the earth or feeding other micro-organisms.

We also consume water and continually passing it off back into the environment via perspiration as we play sport or participating in vigorous activities.

We can see the steam of our breath as we breathe in colder climates; urine and waste are also evidence.

But because we predominantly function from our five senses, we give little or no thought as to what happens to it when it leaves our system, again I know this may be a little graphic for some, depending on our conditioning, but it is fact and I can't change facts unfortunately only state them.

The waste we give off is predominately via the toilet system and is flushed away, and we have the out of sight out of mind mentality.

Usually this may be recklessly sent to a processing plant and then on into the ocean.

I say recklessly as I would take this opportunity to add, the ocean is the earths liver and is being loaded with billions of litres of this effluent on a daily basis.

Personally, each of us are entitled to an opinion be it right or wrong, I would prefer to see it pumped in land where mother nature along with our expertise, could utilise it further for bio-fuels and the solids turned into fertilisers for farming activities, nutrients for the soils of which we farm vigorously, so vigorously we are depleting the soils of the natural nutrients we give off and again, pump into the oceans.

Footnote: we only have to see the growth around septic tank run off, as to how healthy the growth from that is as natural evidence that surpasses all the scientific jargon that give us permission to dump it into the oceans!

We as the earth's population, via the evaporation precipitation of the planets water systems, are sharing each other's fluids and have been doing so, and will continue to do so for billions of years.

Whether we choose to acknowledge or accept this fact is entirely up to each individual, again, I can't change the facts only state them so I make no apologies, we are all one entity, one energy, universe = uni (1) verse (song).

Water, something we take for granted is also a living organism, the next chapter may prick the interest and curiosity a little further.

Water is a living organism

It has also been discovered by Japanese scientist Dr Masaru Emoto that water responds to positivity and negativity.

During his studies Dr Emoto has actually witnessed the molecular structure of water responding to comments either written or spoken and it doesn't matter in which language or dialect.

I would find this difficult to comprehend as a youngster and very sceptical of this notion up until now.

Dr Emoto discovered that when water is exposed to loving comments, the molecular structure takes on a beautiful crystal snow flake appearance, observed and photographed under a high powered microscope.

Also, when water is exposed to high powered emotions of hatred, with statements like, "I hate you!", "your ugly!" or "I'll kill you!"

The molecules took on a very septic appearance. In his book "Living Water" Dr Emoto has actually posted photographic evidence of the various molecular changes to the associated statements.

Given some thought to it, it all made sense to me.

How we feel with different comments and emotions we are exposed to, an example of this is, when we are told we are beautiful, and that "I love you", we feel a warmth flush through our bodies!

This would be what Dr Emoto is saying about the molecules changing to the crystal like snow flake appearance, we can actually feel this taking place within us.

Similarly, when someone says something like "your ugly", I'll kill you", "I can't stand to be near you" we feel a flush of anger and resentment toward the source of comment.

We can all relate to moments like this where we have experienced that warm flush or flash of anger in an instant, so what Dr Emoto has discovered holds credence, sometimes we can even see instant colour changes within persons.

It may also be suffice to say, if we were to hold onto hatred and anger for long periods of time, during the water with in's septic state, could be the ignition of many of our current health challenges, hence the term "laughter being the best medicine" creating chemical changes within.

Medicine explains that the body fills with endorphins during laughter, which is the catalyst for healing; just maybe the endorphins also help purify the septic water within also.

I am not a scientist, just using some logic.

If we choose to take a moment and ponder what we have just read, we will soon begin to understand there is nothing that has ever existed or going to exist that the water on this planet and floating around in our atmosphere, hasn't passed through one species or another in many and various ways for the billions of years our universe has existed.

Some could and may argue, what I am saying is purely speculative, and that's fine, again everyone is entitled to their opinion and I respect that.

Some may argue a case for banning cremation of the human body if this were to be true in what I am saying, and return to the old method of returning the body to the earth.

Again it matters not as to how we dispose of the capsule our energy/soul resides in, the sun rays penetrate the earth to the core, drawing from it all forms of moisture from the great depths just as it has done for billions of years and will continue to do so for who knows how long?

Now, if all that I have been saying is fact, then it would be fair to say the living molecular structure of the water that has and is continually passing through our bodies today, has passed through the bodies of Christ, Budda, Krishna, Allah and the list of all the great avatar's who have passed before us.

It would also be fair to say it has also passed through Adolph Hitler, Saddam Hussein and many other perceived tyrants the world has seen come and go!

Our conscious mind or ego mind, **ego** equals **E**dging **G**od **O**ut, would activate our denial sense, maybe telling us "well the water that passed through them, hasn't passed through me."

To think this way would be wishful thinking, being in denial, being ignorant of the fact that we are all one entity, we are all a part of something amazingly massive, and no one and no thing thrives or survives without water.

The water that has nourished all of the people I have mentioned, has also nourished the bodies and structures of every growing living moving (and what we perceive not to be moving in mountains or stone) creature's, plants and animals.

Everything includes everything, even our cars require water, machinery, everywhere we look or turn water has passed and continues to pass and be consumed, returned and recycled for billions of years.

And will do so for billions of years to come as we are evolving as much as some groups wish to stop us evolving, for this to happen the universe must in turn die!

Again, if this a fact and by now if we haven't yet arrived at this conclusion that it may be a fact (God bless us) wouldn't it be safe to say that everything is and has been linked since the beginning and still is and will be till the perceived end.

Why then do some still choose to ignore, continue to harm, destroy, hate and kill one another, or kill anything if it is essentially a part of each and every one of us?

Those of us who choose to ignore the truth, the facts, and we have them roaming the planet, suicide bombers, are one example who are trained to conform to the likes of an Osama Bin Laden, who could have been likened to that of a cancer cell in the human body, which thinks it must kill all other cells around it in order for its own survival.

In actual fact it is unwittingly destroying itself in the process.

There are no winners with this mindset, seeing ourselves as separate entities when clearly we are not.

We cannot think we can destroy everything and everyone and think we can survive.

There is not one child born into this great planet/universe made from love and nurtured with love as it grows, that would have an agenda to kill and hate, it has to be trained this way.

I remember as a kid growing up, we used to play with our pets, play games like mothers and fathers.

We were introduced to the health systems for inoculation against polio or other diseases we would play doctors and nurses etc.

As we got older we began reading comics, Disney cartoons that used to bring us joy, then came the war comics, so we would start playing soldiers and war games.

Then onto the movie theatre's to watch cow boys fighting and killing over land etc. and so it was, learning to kill, fight and hate, separate and segregate.

Today it is said that the average child is exposed to over ten thousand simulated murders in its own living room by the age of twelve years.

Now with the violent X/box games this may only be increased probably tenfold as we the parent perceptively struggle to make ends meet using the X/box as a baby sitter, we make poor choices only to see things worsen and we wonder why?

The child actually does the killing with the X/box and because it can kill the same person day in day out, becomes desensitised to violence.

We attract it, we create it, our kids suffer, they grow up with their heads filled with all this negativity, we look around to see who we can blame, when we only have to go as far as the nearest mirror to find the cause.

Every time we purchase a violent video/video game, read or watch violence through any media, we are contributing to it, we demand it, so the media supply it, we are the cause, and media is effect.

The other side of the spectrum

On the other side of the spectrum, we have the people who attract wealth and prosperity to themselves, these people by their own choice, share their wealth and prosperity with the perceived less fortunate.

One who comes to mind immediately is Mr Bill Gates, one of the founding members of Microsoft computer software.

It never ceases to amaze me to think there are people who support him by buying his product, and at the same time condemn his success and what he stands for, and there are people who subconsciously live this way sadly.

The American government tried in vain to pull apart the Gates empire, thank God Mr Gates never had the mindset of an Osama Bin Laden, they would have had cause for concern for the planet.

Unlike Bin Laden, Gates cares about people, pays massive payroll taxes, directly and indirectly employ's millions of people, and at this point is a director of his own charity, an organisation who screens charities requesting his wealth to assist the perceived poor and disadvantaged.

This organisation employs people to give his money away, yet governments sort to control him, why?

Fear of an individual having so much wealth is my only guess, as governments need to control

There are many, many people like Gates, the beautiful Oprah Winfrey also gives because not only can she, she not only wants to, she actually loves giving.

Oprah began as each and every one of us began "enter the world with nothing!" not even a wealthy family to start her off, and if we do a little research, we will find this amazing woman had what many of us could call a fairly ordinary start in life, yet she continually chooses to give love and wealth unconditionally to the less fortunate.

By doing this she actually attracts love and wealth back to herself, *"THE LAW OF ATTRACTION"* is clear and concise.

What you give unconditionally, without any expectation we never hear her say "I gave you that so now you owe me!"

It must come back tenfold, Ms Winfrey is a magnificent example of how we should strive to live and become.

On the other hand, we have Mr Bin Laden who gave hatred and killing, and consequently lived the life of a pauper toward the end.

Attracted to himself, what he predominately thought or feared would happen to him.

We have people Like Oprah Winfrey, Bill Gates, Warren Buffett and Ellen DeGeneres, Donald Trump; I could go on and on Richard Branson, who give love joy and happiness along with their wealth.

They attract more of it back to themselves; they can't help it there is no exception, why? Because this is the way they think, and the joy and emotions of giving, making someone happy creates a vacuum, bringing them more to give.

So if we all have a choice, and we all have, there are no exceptions to this, which choice are we going to make?

Which life would you choose?

Something like Osama *Bin* Laden?

Or lives like a Gates or Winfrey who are free to travel at will?

I think the answer would be quite clear for me; I would love to tour the world at will helping and bringing joy into the lives of others, than have to hide away from it like a rat.

Some may question or state that it's all well and good for Gates, Winfrey and Co to give money away, as they are lucky enough to be wealthy enough to be able to do so.

And I would suggest looking at the bigger picture; these people have come from very, very humble beginnings.

Like the rest of us, born with nothing, and at the end of the day will cross back over to our energy source with exactly the same as the rest of us "with nothing" it's what we do between when we arrive and depart that really matters.

Unlike Mr Bin Laden, who was also born with nothing like the rest of us, his parentage were very wealthy.

He never had the struggles of the above mentioned, so I would suggest didn't hold the respect for life, people and humble beginnings the way Mr Gates and Ms Winfrey experienced, hence the contrast in lifestyles unfortunately for Bin Laden.

Life is a game

It's often stated that life is a game, and this is a fair statement, like a chosen sport, its how much we put into it, as to what we get out of it.

There are those who excel, those who are good and those who are average.

Again everything is a choice, some will argue as to how disadvantaged they are because of their circumstances and hard luck stories and say "how could I have attracted the circumstances I am in?

I never asked for this!"

There is a guy, Nick Vujicic, he has been on television.

Nick was born with no arms or legs, how more disadvantaged could we think one could get?

Nick Vujicic is a motivational speaker who so loves life, happy and very positive about life and an inspiration beyond belief.

Mr Vujicic also claims he had two choices, one to feel sorry for his circumstances and seek pity for himself, or make light of his circumstances and get on with life.

Actually doctors even recommended his mother abort him when they realised the extent of his deformities.

Thank God for this amazing woman that she chose not to.

This amazing gentleman took the second choice, that being, to become an inspiration to the rest of us, and that is "no matter what the circumstances, no matter what life deals up" everything comes down to **how we process our thoughts.**

Nick is so grateful for the gift of his perceived disadvantages to inspire others, to have the faith, trust and love within them to make the most of what life presents us.

I am sure he has his moments of down times, but knows how to make the choice of not dwelling upon them.

Like the champion sports person, we see the elite sports person may think "oh they are/were just gifted and brush it off.

Really, it's just another excuse for our not succeeding.

We don't see the passion, drive and effort they put in to attract the success they get as they flow and ooze with seemingly nonchalant ease at what they do.

Its' really a simple metaphor for those of us who drive a car, ride a pushbike or even walk for that matter

Who was a total confident expert the very first time they sat behind the wheel, hopped upon a bicycle or stood up?

But after the first twelve months we get along the road thinking about what we are going to be doing on the weekend or whatever.

Have we ever given any thought as to who or what is driving the car when our thoughts are elsewhere?

This same energy that is beating our hearts, filling our lungs with air, digesting our food is also driving our car when our minds are elsewhere while we seemingly move along in auto pilot.

With the previous examples of success and averages, we can see that *we have the choice* to be either a total success or totally average.

We are the ones making our every choice, what we put out there, we get back, there's no question **"THE LAW OF ATTRACTION"** always works with us.

What we think about we bring about 365 24/7 the Mohammad Ali's (Cassius Clay) Michael Jordan, Tiger Woods, Bill Gates, Oprah Winfrey we can throw in another mentor I follow, world renowned life coach Anthony Robbins.

All have the same thing in common and that is unbending faith, trust and confidence in their chosen fields, go with the flow, always give, and **give with gratitude**, having an unbending love and passion for what they do, and the source of all energy gives them everything they need to succeed.

And so to, it will give us everything we need to succeed or fail if that's the way we predominately feel and see ourselves.

There is simply no-end to learning, there are new encounters, new experiences confronting us in every moment of every day and we must deal with them, with our thoughts and actions continuously.

No beginning, no end

I was fortunate enough to be with my father as he passed away (or crossed over into the next phase of life or returned from whence we came) commonly referred to as death or departing.

Just hours before my father took his last physical breath, he and I were having a discussion about nothing specific, something related to my work, and he made the statement "oh, I didn't know that could be done, that's amazing!"

The point here being, my father at seventy six years of age and me living by my conscious mind, I had the perception that dads knew everything.

I had just come to the realisation, one, we don't know everything, and two, what he always used to tell me, "son we are always learning something new right up until the day we die!" he proved this to me physically.

His quote at the time of our discussion "that he didn't know that!" really drove home the point to me, with a practical demonstration all be it in his death bed, of what he had been trying to teach me all the preceding years we are learning until we take our last breath "THANKS FOR THE INVALUABLE LESSON DAD!

And may I add to this chapter, since I am in father mode, as stated earlier, my father's beliefs in his mind being an Atheist, in his words *"son I don't believe in life after death, "no bastard"* (always straight to the point my dad) *has ever come back and told me there's a life after death!"* and he quipped, *"I'm sure if there were, my mother, father, sisters or brothers would have come and told me so!"*

My father was a very opinionated man and many would say arrogant, set in his ways and I am sure still is, he simply wouldn't have noticed any signs my grandparents, aunties and uncles would have been trying to give him, and in fact he proved that by not seeing any of the so called coincidental occurrences or indications.

As everything in this universe is now scientifically proven to be waves of energy, and this includes us, I will endeavour to dip into this subject just a little to feed the curious mind with something else exciting to mull over.

Because I've already stated "there is neither beginning nor end to anything", this must also include our lives as well as we know it.

As we know and many can attest to this, my father would deny any relationship to being spiritual in any way shape or form, he also knew that I was in some sorts, heading down the spiritual path, he tried on many occasions to steer me in the other direction.

So if he were able to get through to me that his spirit was in fact still around, he would be able let me know in one way or another, also I could and one day will get around to writing a book on this subject and all the experiences I have encountered and am still encountering with my dad and now others, it was very daunting at first and surreal, these days I am more open to and having fun with it.

Just while we are in this area of infinite life, here is a little something for you to ponder, science now has concrete proof that every cell of our body "dies" and is replaced with another in continuous activity, and over a two year period, we have essentially replaced our entire body.

Physical evidence of this phenomenon actually happening is, our hair continually grows no matter how often we cut it back or shave it off, most men shave daily!

We have a continual need to cut our finger and toe nails, if we get sun burned, our skin peels and regrows without us having to purchase any new skin.

Women produce and eliminate unfertilised eggs on a monthly basis.

I personally donate blood plasma platelets every month to assist or share my health with others and the platelets regenerate without my needing to purchase or search for new ones.

This is what we are aware of with our five senses.

Science is now telling us, we replace our liver every six weeks, our skeletal frame every few months, our eyes every forty eight hours or so, our stomach lining every six days.

We could go on and write a whole book on the subject, and again I will as soon as I have this one out there.

But if this is fact, and I have no doubt it is, then if we have lived for twenty years, this essentially means we have completely out lived our bodies ten times!

As I am approaching my sixth decade, this would mean I have out lived my entire body thirty times!

I can also remember things I did as a toddler, so if my body changes out every cell and atom of my make-up, what is it that never dies?

The answer that springs to mind is consciousness, the invisible part of us, memory which sometimes is referred to as the soul.

Just because we can't see it, doesn't mean it doesn't exist, we can't see television signals until we switch the television on and tune in, but we know it's there.

We can't see electricity until we switch the power on or touch live wires, but we know it's there.

Wo can't hear the music or radio commentary either, but we know without a shadow of doubt that if we switch the radio on, it's going to be there.

So where are the radio signals and television when we are not turned on and tuned into them?

The answer to that question must be that they are there, and given that, it could just be feasible for the souls/spirits of the dearly departed are there also, it's just that most of us cannot tune into them, where some psychics and mystics can.

Having ascertained this fact, then it is fair to say that the energy that is my true being that which resides within the cells and atoms that makes up the body temple/vessel is a never ending energy.

It is also an intelligent thinking energy, an energy that we are all a part of which will be explained more as we delve further into this book, but for now, just something extra for us to ponder, and think about.

Gradual opening up to the truth

Opening up to spirituality has been for me, a very gradual process, and I thank God for that, that it has.

It would be easy to see how those who are truly deeply spiritually aligned or enlightened, are generally labelled by the masses as "nutters" or "lunatics" etc.

Because they/we can see things from a totally different perspective and don't worry, I am as guilty as the next person for applying those labels upon others but not anymore.

Remember, whether I was raised Atheist and hypocrite or not, I unashamedly admit it, I now see things much differently these days.

The Christ's and Buddha's more recently Gandhi of India were all seen as different than those who conformed with the masses, but in fact were no different than the rest of us other than living "by choice" from the subconscious mind or the sixth and seventh sense.

These people chose to live connectedly with the source of all creation, they chose to see the greater picture of everything, something each and every one of us is capable of, if we so choose to do so, remember, everything is by choice.

Christ was apparently quoted as once saying, "All people have the ability to achieve what I can achieve, and even greater things than I"

How true was this?

Jesus could place his little ass onto the back of an ass and travel from village to village.

Today we can pop our ass into a vehicle/motor bike, push bike, train or whatever and move from town to town, city to city or place our bottom in a seat on an aeroplane and fly from country to country, or on a ship and sail around the world.

We have the technology to replace hearts and livers, limbs etc.

So yes, this great man knew way back then that anything is achievable, and the power to this point is "IF YOU PUT YOUR MIND TO IT" And what is our mind? **A thought**! And where does a **thought** come from?

Certainly not from inside our head which was at one time perceived to be the case.

More importantly, everything we take for granted today was all available to the cave man; the trees were there, the minerals for everything metallic was patiently sitting in the ground.

The fuels were waiting to be tapped etc.

And again it's sufficed to say that everything we need for the future is also available to us right now as well.

We just have to put our minds onto what it is we really want, and follow our intuition/prompts and move forward with the confidence that we can achieve it.

Footnote; here's a funny thought, we now know that when we physically die, or cross back, our energy exits the physical to return to the source of our energy.

Coronial doctors remove the brains of perceived madmen mass murderers and the like to study the brain to see what made them tick, and in turn, it drives them mad because they can't find the root cause in what's physically left behind.

Who says "God" hasn't got a sense of humour, someone searching for something that's no longer there?

The most important thing we can all learn from the great wise sages of the past, is that they were all humble.

Not one of them sought credit for anything.

They all lived from love and compassion and care for fellow man.

We all still have it within us, the largest majority of us do, some of us appear to have lost the faith but holding onto faith is vitally important.

There are some self-professed spiritual "guru's" of segregated groups (the Taliban) is one such group that springs to mind, terrorists who claim to be spiritual, yet are so far removed from the love of their spiritual teacher Mohammad or Allah, who as their chosen "God" would, I suggest be saddened by their behaviour of killing and trying to control in his/her spiritual name.

Mohammad wasn't a Muslim.

Muslim is the label someone created off of his teachings, as is the same with Jesus Christ not being a Christian.

Christianity was built off of his teachings and neither was Gautama Buddha a Buddhist.

They are all just labels some organisations have formed which has now socially conditioned and gone further away from what these amazing people were trying to teach and were totally, gratifyingly connected too.

Again, as we're all breathing and recycling the same air, we're all drinking and recycling the same water, we cannot separate ourselves from this undeniable fact.

The sun warmed their place on earth as it does almost everyone.

I say "almost" everyone else's, the Eskimo's may dispute this.

If we all share these things and there is no way that we cannot, why then do we think we are all separate entities?

Claiming and maintaining an "I'm right and your wrong" attitude, we are all in his together, and the only way we can bring peace to this planet, is to bring it in together!

One cannot kill the brother/sister of another and then expect the families to love one.

It's been tried over centuries and never been achieved, trying to create peace with anger and hatred is akin to trying to create virginity with sexual intercourse.

An insurmountable task, not completely impossible, if we create another miniature human from that unison.

When we choose to live a separate life, a life of separateness and hatred toward one another, how long can mankind survive?

If everyone chose to become Muslims tomorrow, how would these extremists survive, who could they trust then if they can't trust now?

Remember these are trained, conditioned killers, who would they kill then?

Saddam Hussein, if we can believe what the government and media fed us, trusted no-one, Adolph Hitler was another and more recently Maummar Gaddafi.

Had they not attracted their own return to spirit source, would they have ended up the last people on earth?

Pure madness to the extent they never even trusted their own family.

The evidence is there that the **"Law of Attraction"** worked for them.

They trusted no-one and tried to control the thoughts of other's, a totally impossible task, no-one can choose the thoughts of another.

All these sad tyrants were focused upon or worried about was who they could trust?

Who would be trying to kill them?

All the time sadly, attracting to themselves their own miserable demise, having to live the lives of vermin.

How happy and joyful an existence would that be (don't even try contemplating that one) unless one wishes to attract a vermin life.

Let's pray they all make a better go of it next time around.

From the negative to positive

Moving on form the negativity side of the **"LAW OF ATTRACTION"** although negativity has its place, as we wouldn't understand positivity without it.

The whole universe is a dichotomy (an equal and an opposite) i.e. we have hot and cold, wet and dry, up and down, man and woman, light and dark, quiet and loud.

The only thing that can't be split is silence and the number zero, if we split zero we still have zero, if we split silence we only have more silence.

There is no variance with silence and this is where we go to eliminate the chatter within our conscious mind during meditation etc., more about that a little later on.

So let's take a look at most of metaphoric sayings, "love attracts love," "money attracts money," "success attracts success," "success just seems to follow him/her around," "she/he was born with a silver spoon in their mouth,"

We have heard all or some of those sayings at one time or another without giving much thought as to why it always seems to happen to the others and not to me!

Well people who know me would beg to differ.

I'm always being told how "lucky" I am, or everything I touch turns to gold etc.

I can assure you it hasn't always been this way, we have all had our fair share of challenges along the way and still do.

I just learn to approach challenges a little more light-heartedly these days, and with a little practice we all can.

Every successful person I have had the pleasure to interact with all seemed to have had challenges in life of some sort at one time and another, they still do of cause.

But how do they seem to always recover so quickly?

Well once we learn to basically act like them (think like them) we then seemingly **"ATTRACT"** like them!

It's that simple, sounds too easy don't it?

But I ask how difficult is it to think?

First and foremost we must develop a very powerful love for our self, yes deeply "love one self!"

Believe me this can be difficult, our **"ego"** mind, or the **"devil"** mind, the conscious mind will tell most of us that, "that's bullshit!" the ego mind holds us back and will destroy us if we allow it too.

One example of this I had when working within the mining industry was when a work colleague asked me "who do you place first in your family, yourself or your family?"

Without hesitation I replied, "always myself!" and before I could follow with an explanation, his over powering ego blurted in with, "well I think you're a selfish bastard!" and that he always placed his family first!"

But the fact I tried to explain to him was, "if I don't look out for myself first, and say, I get injured, my family will be burdened with the task of caring form me.

As I am seen as the bread winner in the family, my priority must always be to look after myself first, and then I can bring to my family everything they need!"

This then changed his perception, not only of me, but how he went about his work as well.

The whole culture of the place we worked at began to change, you see, we are all in this "UNI-VERSE" the one song, and if we all care about ourselves, to be the best we can be, we can then bring harmony into our environment and care for each other.

This is my ultimate goal; we don't have to fight and hate to be the best.

We can never gain power over another, we can only ever be the best we can be, and the rest takes care of itself.

The same goes for attracting wealth, if we have perceptions that the wealthy are greedy, we need to change this thought process around very quickly for us to become prosperous as well.

Every person loves to give in one form or another, be it to family or friends, now the point here is, the more we have, the more we have to give, very simple.

And of cause, when we give, we make others feel good, that in turn makes us feel good, and when we feel good, we want more of the same, so if we feel good about giving, and this is vitally important, not expecting anything in return… **"THE LAW OF ATTRACTION"** gives us more to give.

And on and on it goes, again, if we learn to feel good about giving the whole world will then become prosperous.

Receiving is as gracious as giving

We must always just as graciously receive as well; this is just as important as giving.

If someone offers you a gift, be it a million dollars or a half rotten apple, we must receive it with gratitude no matter what.

If we refuse anything, we are saying to **"THE LAW OF ATTRACTION"** I don't want!

Remember the subconscious mind cannot see, it just responds to the information/thoughts we feed into it.

Also be reminded, that the **"source of our energy"** is giving continuously 24/7 – 365 (366 on leap years) and does not discriminate, the example here is the air we breathe.

It doesn't say, well I will rest on Sunday or Saturday, and that all depends on which religion you may or may not be associated with.

Or does it say, today, I will only supply oxygen to the Muslims because they prayed harder this week than the rest, the rest can go without.

If our source were to take the day off, the world would stop spinning, the sun wouldn't shine, there would be no air to breathe, our hearts would stop beating, birds wouldn't be able to fly (we could go on forever)

If we all made a conscious effort to firstly learn to love ourselves unconditionally and then send that love out to everything and everyone, the world would automatically become a much joyous place to live in.

Sometimes I hear the rumblings of how could that happen?

Well we don't have to look far.

Nelson Mandela immediately comes to mind, what a wonderful example of loving forgiveness this great man is, just recently celebrating 20+ years of freedom, having been incarcerated for 27 years for wanting to live as equally as anyone else basically.

He even invited his former jailor to the celebration, not to gloat over his victory for freedom and peace, but purely as an act of forgiveness for what must have been years of torment.

He could have been forgiven for being bitter about it all.

Mr Mandela is such a gracious example of a human being we could all strive to match, who would have thought that this once labelled rebellious criminal would be released from prison to become the most gracious humble leader of his own country?

Evidence that love is more powerful than hatred, a lesson all the worlds so called leaders could follow.

If we take a snapshot of how **"THE LAW OF ATTRACTION"** worked in Mr Mandela's life, in the early rebellious part, he was rebelling **"AGAINST"** apartheid, so he was very emotional, very passionate about his cause, so much so, he was actually attracting more anger toward himself at that time.

Fast forward a few years, being in solitary confinement, Mr Mandela had thinking time, quiet time or can we go one further **"SILENT"** time.

The time to hear the subconscious mind offer to him, not only solutions in his endeavour to have his people being treated as equal, but for him to lead compassionate change.

People were expecting blood to be shed for him seeking his revenge, from all countries around the globe, but he was working with a greater power.

Mr Mandela, utilised the awesome power he had gained by reconnecting with the source of all creation to not only lead the people of his country, but also become one of the most revered and respected people on the planet today.

May I take this opportunity to say THANK YOU NELSON MANDELA for being a guiding light and a wonderful example for me personally to model myself upon?

Where there is hatred, let me sow love" from the prayer of St Francis of Acisi.

Love undoubtedly, has more power than hatred, the evidence of this is so overwhelmingly obvious.

We all remember or have heard of Jesus Christ, but who remembers the name of the person who actually drove the spikes into the hands and feet of Christ?

Not who requested it (Ponchos' Pilot) but who actually performed the act of hatred.

When Mr Mandela **MADE THE CHOICE** to forgive firstly himself and then those who chose to incarcerate him, his personal power became absolute.

The evidence is, it happened in our lifetime.

He chose to forgive and love, so *"ATTRACTED"* love and forgiveness into his life and the lives of those who chose to befriend him.

"The Law of Attraction"

We have come this far and by now I feel sure you may be beginning to realise there is much more going on around us than we had previously realised.

For some, they already know this, and will find this book as re-enforcing what they have already learned and seeing it from someone else's perspective can be refreshing as well as assuring.

As we are now beginning to understand what is already scientifically proven, it is evident that the whole universe is entirely made up of a vibrational energy (frequency waves)

As with radio and television waves, our thoughts are emitting a frequency which is tuned into this energy field and passes out into the universe to who knows where.

And, is eventually a return to us as to what we perceive physical form.

So loving is our source energy, the stronger the emotion (perceived asking) the faster and quantity it is returned to us, be it in the negative or the positive.

It matters not to our universal source, again as it cannot see, it always assumes we are asking for more of it and lovingly and unconditionally obliges.

I hear people saying "well I sure as hell didn't ask for the cancer" or "I am sure no one asked for the volcano eruption, earthquake and so on.

Without having all the answers or explanations as to why these mass phenomena's happen, we do have examples of one couple who were caught up in the London train station bombing, deciding to move to Queensland Australia only to be caught up in the mass flooding, then moved to New Zealand right into the massive earthquake which struck Christchurch, seemingly moving from one disaster to another.

As we watch these happenings through the many media outlets, we discuss them with others, feeling the emotions within the moment.

Without realising we are subconsciously attracting similar circumstances to us, and because they don't happen instantly we have no correlating thoughts as to whether we have actually attracted them or not.

Recently we witnessed a young person who got to meet her idols, pop band One Direction.

This young woman excitedly explained to the media she had posters on her bedroom wall for around twelve months.

Dreamed of meeting them and had very powerful emotions of hysterical love for the group, she was selected by a local media crew who were amused by her babbling excitement of having a chance to at least see her idols in the physical.

So emotional was this young woman, she found herself being invited to have a hug with the members of the group and the next day received two free tickets to see her idols perform live.

This brought a tear of joy to my eye, simply because I could see all the events unfolding that had her attracting all this to herself, her friend and media just fobbed it off as "luck".

We don't need or have to take my word for this happening, as there are a multitude of books, audio books, dvd's and other documented evidence out there who support what I am saying and having read this book, the chances are now you will be attracting more of this information to you.

Just as you have attracted this book, now your subconscious mind will search and find more material of a similar trait.

And with the amazing technology Google etc. it is more accessible today than it was when my awakening started some twenty years ago, accelerating your learning if this is your wish.

Rarely do we receive recognisable circumstances

When we begin trying to manifest ideal things into our lives, very rarely do we recognise we have achieved what it is we feel we've wanted until we become more familiar with it.

Usually it's only when we look back can we identify or correlate the circumstances initially.

A wonderful example of this is of a teacher in manifesting what you want, John Assaraf, who used the power of visualisation to attract the house of his dreams.

John use to be a street gang member during his youth, had placed a picture of a beautiful home he thought he would love for his family.

He used to look at his vision board and imagine living in the home, thinking one day he would love to build one just like it.

Five years later, after moving homes a few times, he actually found himself and his family living within the actual house he had posted on his vision board, not one like it, but the actual house.

John Assaraf, had no idea he and his family had moved into the home until he tried explaining to his five year old son what a vision board was and how it worked, it was only then he realised how the law of attraction had worked for him.

And of course the circumstances be them from fear, joy, anger or very loving, will not always mirror what we experience instantly which makes it difficult to correlate the events that set the wheels of attraction in motion.

Apparently our thoughts and emotions can be measured, and has been measured, discovered by Dr David Hawkins.

Positive emotions are apparently ten thousand times more powerful than negative emotions, which is fantastic because if we catch ourselves out having negative thoughts, we can then switch our thoughts to the positive.

With practice, as with everything, the more we practice anything, the better we become at it.

So turning things around from a downward spiral can be done quite quickly when we know how.

The best way I have found for seeing how I've attracted good and bad circumstances into my life is to sit quietly and take my life back to the earlier thoughts, slowly thinking my life through to the present moment.

It's then I start having these ahhhh moments, it becomes so much easier to place the links of events like placing the pieces of a jigsaw together, the closer we come to the present moment in life from the earliest recollection, it all begins to make sense as it unfolds.

It's pretty much that simple or that complicated, whichever way we choose to look at.

Some of us will always see the glass half full, while others see the glass half empty! We all have differing views and that's the way life has been so magically designed because if we all saw things the same way, we simply wouldn't evolve as a species.

It's the way it's meant to be otherwise there would be no need for political systems, any police, any hospitals or tourism destinations there wouldn't be any reason for human beings to exist.

Vibration

Everything is vibration, the whole universe; everything is continual movement. The most notable things we see moving are the oceans, rivers, the swaying of trees and grass in a breeze, birds flying, people walking running etc. traffic and on and on we could go.

It may also appear some things are not moving at all, such as the ground we walk upon, mountains, buildings etc. etc. but I assure you that everything is vibrating at varying speeds.

Mining is moving mountains as do earth tremors, volcanos and sometimes if we are in a building where air traffic flies close we can feel or hear things in the building move.

In the earth, we have worms and ants other insects and bacterium which we can't see with the naked eye all moving around at varying speeds, everything is in continual motion the landscape is in continual change.

Creatures are burrowing, farmers are turning the soil, roads are being built, excavations are happening on one side of the world while the other areas sleep, and even then we have nocturnal creatures (as well as nocturnal humans being shift workers)

People and animals are being born and dying, at varying stages of life in a continuum of endless activity.

All this is happening as we are unconsciously hurtling through space at thousands of kilometres/miles per hour and have been for billions of years.

Most of us are consciously oblivious to all this activity as we busy ourselves arguing which religion is right or wrong (we have wars about it) which sporting team is the best or blissfully making love!

What organises all this?

Energy

Everything in this universe is energy, the very thoughts we think are energy, when we need to go to the bathroom/toilet, we get a transmission from the control centre or command centre or God.

It tells us we need to eliminate waste, and this is triggered by an electrical impulse from a pressure point within the bladder or the bowel which transmits to the brain and as we are programmed/conditioned to, we move in auto pilot to where we need to go and do what we need to do without giving a second thought as to all the systems that fire up every muscle for us to move.

Every muscle to make every step move our arms, neck, head etc. as we move to go anywhere, all with amazing synchronicity, every pressure point, every cell within ever muscle sending electrical impulses through thousands of nerve endings to the brain in rapid succession, truly amazing.

Trillions of things are happening simultaneously within the universe and within our bodies.

We are creating new blood cells, new muscle cells, digesting food, incubating babies, driving a car or swimming, playing sport, eliminating waste fighting illness all at the same time, how does all this happen?

What coordinates all this?

If all this energy is happening within us and scientifically proven that energy cannot be destroyed or created, we cannot wet it, we cannot blow it up, all are forms of energy, then where does this energy go when we supposedly die?

Money is a form of energy in continual vibration, movement, again at varying speed, we can hoard it and think or believe it is stationary, occasionally we may get it out and count it, we put it in the bank and do you think for one minute that, that is where it sits until you draw it out?

Banks keeps a record of how much you have and then distribute it to whom and who knows where?

Again when we think we hoard our money, we supposedly die, someone else receives it and off it goes again.

The coins are minerals mined from the ground, the paper money was once a tree, and plastic money is a by-product of petro chemicals drilled and extracted from the earth.

We really don't notice or try to understand the bigger picture as we are usually too occupied as to what is going on directly around us living and functioning from our five senses.

This is totally fine but in a way sad because we are in effect totally ignoring the pure potential for which each and every one of us have for us to tap into, the successes we were born to have.

The clothes on our backs are also a form of energy, made to keep us warm since we have evolved from wearing predominately animal skins, to animal fur, to plant life (cotton and hemp) everything that has ever been made, first there has been preceded by a **thought**, and what is a **thought**, its energy!

Great, now we're getting it.

First comes the thought, and then something moves, and in most instances, people, events and circumstances are moved to ensure what it is that's thought about is actually brought about.

At this point I am not going to get into the scientific terminology, I just wish to speak in every day terms, but briefly, we are made up of atoms, particles, subatomic particles and now they have recognised something called photons which are the makeup of intelligent magnetic matter.

This matter, when a thought is given to what it is we desire, magnetically are drawn together to manifest into the object we desire, like the illusion of the magician.

And once it has been created is this the end?

No, no matter what has been created, it can be improved upon, take the automobile for instance, look at how much improvement has come since the first automobile to what we have today.

Where will the evolution of the automobile end?

It won't, I would envision one day in the not too distant future, we will have energy efficient vehicles that may have nuclear energy installed during the manufacturing stage that will last the life of the vehicle.

We may be able to by-pass nuclear energy altogether with perpetual motion, the turning of the wheels creating electricity charging battery cell implanted in the panels, I don't really know, I'll leave that one to the experts, but it is happening now.

We will be able to program our destination and it will take us there sensing and avoiding all vehicles, obstacles and maintaining correct speed limits, accidents will become a thing of the past, it's all possible.

Remember, everything we have today was available to the cave man.

So what does the future hold for us?

If we so choose to become smart enough to work through the loving source of energy, which is proven beyond all doubt, to be flowing through each and every one of us, if we all choose to work together as one instead of thinking we are all separate.

The very sun which warmed the butts of Christ and Buddha before him and Mohammad, name them all, is the very same sun that is warming our butts today, there is no question of that.

And when we get this, and cease claiming that what I teach is the right way and go to the extreme of trying to kill another just to prove I'm right, when this couldn't be further from the truth.

There are many now who have chosen to study all religions and getting right to the point or to cut the chase, each religion with all their beliefs and interpretations are all pointing to the one thing, the one song UNI-VERSAL ENERGY one entity, the one and the same, the very thing that's beating my heart, is also beating your heart, there is no escaping the fact, deny it all we like, show me how it's not, I am very keen to learn.

Thoughts

Mike Dooley, author, public speaker and a spiritual teacher off the DVD phenomenon **"THE SECRET"** sums it up with three words **thoughts become things!**

And by now we should be beginning to ascertain this within our own minds. Our thoughts are all a part of this energy, so what we place our attention upon we see more of and it matters not whether it's good bad, happy or sad we simply just get more of it.

A few more examples of this will help our understanding become even clearer.

If we buy a car for instance, we generally search around for something that resonates with us, something we feel good about, something we feel we will look good in.

We find a way to purchase it and are really chuffed once we are inside driving along the road and it usually isn't too long before we see another vehicle which looks identical to the one we have purchased for ourselves.

I have a friend Allan who purchased a silver hummer, and as I explained to him how this all works he commented as to how funny it was that I use this example, because when Allan had purchased his silver hummer, the dealership assured him that he had purchased the only silver hummer in the state.

Allan was as proud of himself as he could be; he had something very unique, the only silver hummer on the road in Tasmania!

He proudly drove off the car lot and into a service station to fill up his gleaming new unique vehicle with fuel.

When he stepped out of his hummer, in behind him pulled up another silver hummer, the same model as his own but bearing interstate number plates, it had arrived that morning on the shipping line.

Now is this a coincidence or just the "law of attraction" at work?

Source energies awesome sense of humour, Allan saw that vehicle a few more times in the passing weeks, I think we can all relate to something of this nature.

We can also walk around shopping centres and not really notice, let's say for this example a washing machine, and as soon as ours breaks down "PRESTO" we then begin seeing washing machines everywhere, so many to choose from we don't really know where to begin.

Now I can hear some saying, "well why doesn't money just show up when we are broke?" and the answer to this is that when we are broke, what we are thinking?

We have no money! and therefore, we are attracting what we're thinking about, **I have no money**, so what does the loving source do?

It sends us more reasons and things to ensure we **have no money!** It's unfailing, it works all the time, and again, you needn't take my word for it, there are many, many authors out there teaching this very subject.

A personal experience of this is when I was struggling in life and following the advice of all the self help teachers, I had absolutely no idea how "The Law of Attraction" worked at the time.

I was following the advice of the teachers and wrote down a fairly substantial amount of money I needed.

I was often asked as to why I needed that much wasn't it greedy to be wanting so much?

I was also asked how I was going to come into this amount of money.

The answer I gave them was always the same, "I don't know how I am going to get it, all I know is that all the self help teachers said I must have a goal or a figure to work toward so this is it, this is what I want!"

Most would just laugh and say "good luck with it then".

Well some time later, a chain letter arrived, just out of the blue it basically had some instructions to follow and I had to send the person at the top of the list of four names, ten dollars and by doing this I would know in my mind that it would work.

Then I was to remove the person at the top of the list, move the other three up and place my name at the bottom of the list of four.

Then I had to make two hundred copies and send them out randomly to two hundred people and wait for the dollars to come in.

Well I personally couldn't see how this wouldn't work, call me gullible, stupid or just plain crazy, but I had sent the person at the top of the list ten dollars, so it had worked for him and if it worked for him, then it must work for me mustn't it?

Anyway to ensure I was putting my name out there, I also (and this is important to digest) **very excitedly and enthusiastically** shared this information with family and friends and assisted them in setting it up for themselves, of course with my name now just above theirs, so yes I knew it was working, ***no doubts at all***.

Now by doing this it had a twofold reason, one was it was ensuring my name was getting out there much faster, and very importantly I was also helping them to generate income for themselves as well, to this day, I still see absolutely nothing wrong with this idea, because if we all gave this practice a go and did it continuously, everyone would have an opportunity to have money come in to purchase things they would otherwise not be able to afford when their turn came.

But the government for many and varied reasons, chose to make it an illegal practice, stating that someone must eventually miss out.

The so called chain letter could do the rounds for an eternity if everyone so chose to play it; it would only be creating opportunities for strugglers to lift their head above financial struggles.

It would be only out of fear of the government missing out on revenue, which it wouldn't as people would be spending freely hence GST. Stamp duty, car registrations, fuel excise taxes would all come into play actually stimulating the economy instead of strangling the economy with poor decision making we see most governments repeatedly making.

Enough of that negative government bashing.

Now, with all the excitement I was feeling, again I couldn't see how this wouldn't work.

I was expecting the dollars to come rolling in, and in around two weeks from receiving this "chain" letter, being very passionate about making it happen, I received a very substantial windfall from an unexpected source.

Was this a coincidence?

At the time I called it luck, everyone did, everyone who knows me keep telling me just how "lucky" I am, how I always seem to land on my feet with virtually everything I do.

It's only when I began learning what I am endeavouring to impart to you right now, when I look back, I can see how everything has so perfectly unfolded, linking all the emotions with the thought processes when these significant events unfolded in my life.

An awakening moment for me

I was exercising one morning just ahead of a planned trip to Sydney when I had an "Ahhhh" moment.

I clearly remember clearly thinking to myself, "*I know how all this works*" then, *how can I teach others about this?*

I was so excited, thoughts began rushing through my mind at a 100miles an hour, but I was off to Sydney to learn options trading with a group of amazing people with whom I had met through the Anthony Robbins foundation.

Upon my arrival in Sydney, a friend of mine, Phil, asked me if I had seen a DVD called **"The Secret"**, to which I had answered I hadn't, asked what it was all about?

Phil explained it to me in basics and during the lunch break, went home to get a copy for me to view, now keep in mind I had this awakening moment at home as to how this all worked and was excitedly trying to figure out how to teach this stuff.

At the end of the day, after our options trading seminar, I retired to my motel room to view this DVD **"The Secret"** and as it began to unfold, I thought, THIS IS IT!

I can assure you being an underground miner and generally a fairly rough house sort of a fella, I have no shame at all in telling you, the tears streamed down my face as I continued to view what I considered at the time, to be an absolute master piece.

So overjoyed was I in that moment, I contacted Phil and asked him how many copies he had?

Phil replied, one dozen, I said, I will purchase them all.

I handed them out to participants in the class claiming, "THIS IS ALL YOU NEED TO KNOW!" but sadly while it is an amazing learning tool being visual and a fairly accurate account of how it all happens, I have since found that there were a lot of pieces missing.

And please don't get me wrong, I am not condemning **"The Secret"** in any way shape or form, it's fantastic, but we can only cram so much in at any given time before we have a brain overload because it really runs against the grain as to how we've been socially conditioned for centuries, generation after generation prior to our coming here.

The narrator of **"The Secret"** the amazing and beautiful Rhonda Byrne has also realised this and has created other tools which have all evolved to help people to create amazing lives for millions of people.

I am a huge fan of her products; in fact I still purchase her products today and give them as gifts to people I see struggling in an effort to help.

This is also why I am writing this book, as we each see things from different perspectives.

In this book, all I am doing is teaching what I have learned from a multitude of amazing teachers, stuff that's already out there and accessible.

I'm explaining it from my perspective and hopefully simplifying the scientific data into everyday social language as I have a very limited standard education so no university jargon, not that standard education is any lower than standard thinking.

If we look at most of today's successful business people, the largest percentage of these people are from a standard educational background, as were most of the most outstanding inventors of our time on planet earth.

I would suggest the reason these people were and are so successful would be the fact that their minds were not overloaded with things that could go wrong, so remain focused on positive outcomes and achieve them.

Not that education is bad, but what we learn is from the past and while that's good, some educational learning has changed by the time the next generation gets to it, but the curriculum hasn't.

Duplicity, media contribution to world events

We see duplicity examples in our lives on a daily basis.

One day we see through varying media outlets and this includes the internet/social media so we are all responsible, violent behaviour in our educational system or on the streets, then within hours, days or weeks we hear, see or hear of similar events.

Then wonder what the world is coming too, it's too easy to just fob it off and blame it as copycat events or behaviours while we are continually advertising and complaining about idiotic behaviour, we are unconsciously contributing to it.

Thousands upon thousands of people viewing simultaneously these kinds of events, are all sending out emotional frequencies and if this is not enough, our media continually repeat footage of violence, tsunami's earthquakes etc. and we wonder why we are continually viewing similar events over and over.

Another example of this is when we witnessed the famous wildlife worrier Steve Irwin who was speared through the heart by a stingray, it's been well documented that Steve, felt and had concerns about moving into an area fairly unfamiliar territory for him, that being the ocean.

Only Steve would have known exactly how much apprehension/fear he may have harboured about moving into this area, but as a bloke, I can attest to the fact that we tend to hide our concerns and emotions. The fact he mentioned he had some nervous energy about the new adventure should give us an indication as to what he may have been attracting.

And while we can ponder as to what Steve may or may not have been feeling, the fact that the event was transmitted around the world at record speed, the pouring out of emotions globally were also televised, a tribute to just how loved and respected Mr Irwin was and still is via his family, friends and many around the world he would never had met or could have imagined loved and cared about him.

Now, what a lot of people may or may not have noticed was, almost exactly a week after the incident with Steve, we had a man on the other side of the world who received a spear through the heart from a stingray.

Only this gentleman had learned the lesson Steve's mishap had to offer, in that, rather than wrenching the barb from his chest/heart as Steve had done, this person cut the tail off the stingray and had it surgically removed.

The question that lingers within me is, how much emotion, thought and imagination did this person use to attract to himself almost so similar circumstances to himself?

Again only this person will ever know as we are the only masters of our thoughts.

The sceptics among us will see these things as just coincidences, I can understand this way of thinking, I used to be a sceptic myself and raised as such, I now see things differently of cause.

One could go on forever and ever giving examples of linking **"the law of attraction"** the fact remains that it is happening in our lives 24/7, 365 days and again 366 on leap years, there are no exceptions.

We can argue what I am saying into eternity as to whether it does or doesn't, be it evidence of it working for us, or we will see it happening in other ways, and if we are searching for evidence that it isn't working for us, we will see the evidence of that as well.

I've lived on both sides of the spectrum and have all the evidence I need and I'm not alone, so I have no reason to argue or do I have a point to prove to anyone.

The fact that we choose not to place a conscious realization upon it, is that, as we read through the media, see it in movies, the news, video games etc. we are feeding our subconscious mind with thoughts, pictures and emotions so it (our subconscious mind) then goes to work on creating similar circumstances and events for us to encounter.

Again, it depends upon how much time, feeling and effort we place upon it as to how quickly it happens in our lives or manifesting it.

You see our subconscious mind can't see, it is blind and can only respond and function off of the information we feed into it.

Once we begin to open our minds up to what I am saying is bearing some truth for you, a whole new world begins to open up, as the saying goes' "change the way we look at things, and the things we look at change!"

Some choose to see the cup half full, while others choose to see the cup half empty!

Change the way we behave around people and the people around us will behave differently; governments could choose to follow the last principle.

Instead of spending around 30 billion of tax payers' dollars training people to enter other countries to train those people to efficiently kill their own kind, then claim they are doing it to protect us from terrorism, if we look at it more deeply, is it protecting us?

Or simply teaching them to hate us, so much so to the extent they feel they must enter our country and blow things up to seek retribution, who are the terrorists?

And if we attract what we think and fear about, can we expect terrorism in our country?

The last question answers itself.

How long do we put up with intruders coming into our back yard either uninvited or invited by a disgruntled family member, come into the yard with the intention of damaging property and or harming other family members?

We can never teach or expect anyone to fall over us with love when we enter their yard with hatred; it's been tried unsuccessfully for centuries and hasn't worked yet! It has been said, "Trying to create peace with hatred", it doesn't work let alone make any sense!" No child is born with the intent to kill another, it has to be trained to do so, and since every child is created from an act of love or a desire to love, hatred is a taught thing.

Goal setting for the greater good

Goal setting for creating a better life for ourselves, firstly we must be totally clear on the fact that we must always place ourselves first and foremost.

When I first heard this, my first thought was that it was being selfish to place oneself ahead of our family and friends.

The reason we must place ourselves first is, we cannot create or manifest for anyone else, that's impossible as we are the one doing the thinking, therefore what we are thinking, we are attracting to ourselves period.

If we wish someone to win the lottery to help them on with life, chances are we will be the ones winning the lottery.

Then if we feel guilty about that, because we were wanting it for someone else, we then in effect begin pushing more good from coming to us, and not only are we feeling for the other persons plight, we are subconsciously attracting similar of those circumstances to ourselves.

Similarly, if we wish someone dead through hatred, ouch! Watch out!

Because what we think about we bring about, so if you are choosing to allow someone to get under your skin and I emphasize **you are choosing** remember no-one else can think our thoughts for us, endeavour to catch the negative thoughts and switch them, and hope the other person finds love and move on with their lives, we will be finding love entering our lives.

Important to get into the habit of thinking, *"all our thoughts have the attractor factor attached to them"*, so always feel and think for an abundance of happiness, health and wealth even to our perceived greatest enemy.

Sure it will be hard to come to terms with at first as our conscious or **EGO MIND** will always be telling us to retaliate at first.

Gautama Buddha was a great exponent of always remaining happy under any circumstances.

When asked, why he remained so kind and loving toward a particular person who had deliberately set out to hurt and upset him over a period of time.

Buddha's reply was simple, "if someone offers me a gift, and I do not accept the gift, then who must the gift belong too?"

That is just so powerful… Essentially we subconsciously react in an expected manner due to our conditioning/programming, very predictable, so if we don't react as expected, who gets upset?

The person trying to control us with intimidation and fear will soon begin to realise they have **"no power"** of control over you and become upset.

Another example of this is when a couple are going through a divorce, the perceived hurt one, will usually hire a lawyer to take the other to the cleaners in an "I'll show you attitude", in an effort to inflict hurt or pain on the other.

A person I know who was in this situation and had worked hard all his life, accumulated a substantial property and financial portfolio, and the partner was choosing to make life difficult for him to inflict the pain.

The partner who had worked day and night to establish their acquisitions didn't wish to fight and bicker so said to the other, you can have it all!

I am not going to make myself ill and some lawyer wealthy, so you take it all!

This action took whatever "perceived" power the other thought they had over the other away in an instant.

In the end it was quickly realised they couldn't control the other or handle all the paperwork associated with changing everything over on their own, and then started to feel the pain they were trying to inflict upon the other, was in fact now becoming very painful for themselves and ended up giving up trying to take it all.

Today after being divorced, they both get on better now than when they were married, the best outcome for both.

By now hopefully with these examples, we are beginning to form a picture as to how "if it is to be, then it has to be up to me!" and this statement stands for everything we wish to achieve out of life.

Again no-one else can think our thoughts, feel our feelings, hurt us, heal us without first having permission from us, so therefore where ever we are at in life, it has always been our choice, apparently we even chose the moment of our conception and I don't doubt that either now.

After reading the book by author Mike Dooley "Manifesting Change" It couldn't be easier; this I can highly recommend.

Mike Dooley states very clearly that in that the use of three words **"thoughts become things"** rings with so much truth, in fact it is the truth, just because we have delays in thinking from what we want, to when we actually manifest things, we don't associate or relate them, especially negative outcomes to thoughts we have had some time ago, sometimes in just moments, sometimes days, weeks, months and even years ago.

With goal setting, Mike, along with most spiritual teachers of today recommend, we think of our desire and feel the emotions as though we have achieved it already, **thinking from the end** and then the people, events and circumstances are moved to ensure the outcome we want is created as we move toward it **taking actions** to achieve our dreams.

The more **emotions** and **excitement** we feel and the more focus and effort we place upon it, the faster it happens.

But it is vitally important for us to follow our intuition and take action, this book hasn't just written itself.

I have read a lot of books, then set about writing and organising the publishing etc. **taking action**.

The late great Walt Disney is a fantastic example of this, and although he passed over, before his last dream become a physical reality, when the project was completed and opened, it was reported in the media that one journalist quipped "isn't it a shame Walt isn't here to see its completion?"

The response from Walt's son was "he saw it long before anyone else!"

Walt Disney was a very passionate man about his desire to bring joy, laughter and happiness to millions of people and he achieved it during his physical life time on this planet.

If today's political systems globally took Walt Disney's philosophy to life in bringing joy to the masses, instead of trying to control everyone and everything, a totally impossible achievement, instead of preaching, gloom and doom by publicly arguing, setting poor examples for our children to follow, spending billions of the public's dollars training our children to what they claim to legally enter another country and murder their civilians.

By following the Disney philosophy, it would not only be bringing joy to millions, it also creates millions of jobs for the masses during construction, then during the running of those kinds of things, tourism dollars flow, and the economy stimulates, none of it is difficult, I mean how difficult is it to laugh and be happy?.

Footnote: Walt Disney reputedly arrived in Hollywood with $40 in his pocket, and today brings joy to millions across the planet, creating hundreds of thousands of jobs and reportedly has a forty billion annual turnover.

The Disney theme song says it all "When you wish upon a star, **and this is important,** makes no difference who you are, all your dreams come true!"

Walt Disney's first venture began with a rabbit and was taken from him by a company partner (I don't know what the company partners name was nor am I interested to find out, but God bless him anyway) but Mr Disney held fast to his dream 'to bring joy to millions" and ***"IT BEGAN WITH A MOUSE!"***

Creating and maintaining the vision

So we have to become clear what it is that we want in life, write it down so it is imprinted in our minds and then draw/ sketch, find a photo of a destination we would love to visit, the body we would love to have or the car of our dreams, or bank statement for that matter, anything we can imagine.

Begin by staring at the picture for a few moments then close our eyes and imagine ourselves being there, apply the emotions, smell the smells, hear the sounds taste the tastes as though we are truly there, remember, the subconscious mind cannot see, it's going on the information we feed into it.

The next step is to see or recognise the prompts and importantly take the appropriate action to ensure it happens.

Then we may come up with all sorts of questions and excuses as to why we can't do it

This is the EGO mind at play, but there is always a way if we desire something truly bad enough.

Timely reminder: As I've explained earlier and it will serve as a reminder here as well, all the greatest names in history, people we all continually speak about with admiration of their achievements.

All of them have served to bring us the luxuries and benefits we experience today, the caveman could never have imagined way back when, were all labelled as eccentric ignorant out of the society stream thinkers in their time.

Thomas Edison, Benjamin Franklin and Christopher Columbus, more recently, Walt Disney, all the champions of humanity and the likes of Christ, Buddha and latter day saints like Gandhi and Mother Theresa.

All ridiculed by main stream socially conditioned masses who resisted or feared reprisals from their perceived so called leaders.

Leaders who actually murdered and crucified some of these people simply to maintain perceived power or control of the minds and potential of the masses, and in doing this, brought about hatred which we have since seen has escalated into wars.

As we all know, each of these champions of humanity, and we all have this potential, were not to be swayed by the masses, which is truly amazing and powerful in itself as they already knew back then what we're truly capable of as history and todays science is revealing with today's technology at an ever increasing speed.

And we still have the sceptics amazingly oblivious as to what is all happening around them, but never mind as I used to be one of them.

The sceptics are just not ready yet and will choose to continue learning life's lessons the hard way, blaming others and circumstances seemingly out of their control God bless them.

It's not a simple concept to grasp at first because we have been programed and hard wired through generations and generations over the centuries of governed teachings, education systems all innocently meaning well, just handing down what they have been conditioned to.

My pathway

I feel it is time to share my pathway to enlightenment, which in fact is continually evolving and will continue right up until I draw my last physical breath and return to the energy of origin.

I am not a religious person, not now, never have been and never will be, religion is a form of tribalism, seeing themselves mostly separate from the mainstream.

I'm not condemning religion pare say, as they have all served humanity for centuries and all point to the one thing we call "God" or "Allah", "the great spirit", our energy source, our higher self, you see it matters not what we call it, we can call it "Fred' or "Jack" it's not blasphemous unless you think it is and punish yourself for it.

Our source won't punish you, it never does and never has, and in fact it so loves and is so giving, if we think we will be punished, we will be, because we will attract it.

And the more pain and sickness we punish into our lives, the more we see/feel it, and the more focus we place upon it, the more our source will give us, it's so loving, the more powerfully we feel it, the greater the quantity and the faster we receive it, good and bad, as it knows no difference contrary to what we have been taught.

And of course each religion truly believes their "God" only really serves them, to the extent they sometimes fight and kill one another which is actually a fear of being wrong, living from the EGO (Edging God Out) please trust now, "God" truly serves us all simultaneously, there is simply no way it (he/she however we choose to see this energy) cannot.

Whereas "Spirituality" as I see it, and I stand to be corrected every reader will have her/his own opinion, separates no one and no thing, it doesn't say to one group, you can have all the air and water, and the others have to purchase it from you, as governments would have us believe, please forgive that comment but I can't help myself or change the facts.

Our source unselfishly and lovingly serves all things equally, everything has an equal and an opposite, whether we think we want it, or whether we think we don't want it, we get it no question; just the quantities vary with the emotions we feel.

I did have a little religion in my life as a child, as my grandfather from my mother's side being a farmer who appreciated the mother earth and all it provided for him, was a religious man and remained so until he left the physical and returned to the source.

So my mother had some religious conditioning she felt compelled to program into her offspring, which was going to be a challenge to her from the outset, remember her offspring had atheist genetics implanted into them "God has an awesome sense of humour", presenting mum with this task.

Mother would send my brother and I off to Sunday school with a small amount of money for the collection plate, this is called **"tithing"** a very important function for "The Law of Attraction" which is something we will get into a little deeper later.

The only value I had for money at that time of my life was that it could be used for more important things than putting food on the plate of some old preacher, when it could be used for the purchase of yummy lollies "please forgive me mum?"

I never realised, well no one had told me back then!

If you tithe, and especially from the heart, with unconditional love without any expectation of anything in return, what you give, returns to you tenfold, hence the reason for tithing 10%, it's like earning ten per cent from the bank on everything you deposit.

So along with my childhood Sunday school excursions and scripture lessons a way of getting out of class and homework during my formative years, which was about all the religion I had.

My father's idea of religion while we were kids, was to tell mum he was taking us for a drive to take us off her hands so she could get the housework done in peace, was to take us for a drive, and oddly enough, every Sunday he would take us out the road to the local football club so he could have a beer with his mates while we waited in the car for him, and we were rewarded with a "hot dog" for our patience and that was the extent of my religious training.

I thought the preacher had a job, just like my dad, no one ever told me why we should give him money when all I thought they were talking about some old dead spirit floating around in some faraway place called heaven.

As a child I really wasn't interested in some old bloke and even dead where he lived or what he was up too, a child's imagination is continually growing and expanding and I believe we totally teach our children everything wrong, spirituality, sexuality and the process of thinking, and unconsciously setting them up for failure in life, this is my perception and again open for discussion and opinion.

Fast forwarding my life, I would have to say, source energy or "God" has always played the part in my life, teaching me lessons as I lurched aimlessly from success to failure, from failure to success, happiness to sadness, sadness to happiness as the vast majority of us do.

Broken relationships, mixing with alcohol and suffering the associated consequences that come with it, loss of driving licence, violence, loss of friendships, looking back, I attracted it all, the good and the bad.

I had made all the choices and received all the consequences, sure at the time I blamed this one and that thing for driving me to drink, but at the end of the day, I was the one who made the choice of tipping it down my throat.

The police and everyone else were just doing their jobs trying to protect me from myself, and protect the public from the behaviours I had chosen to take it's that simple.

Losing a child

I know now looking back, my first spiritual experience or realisation come to me when my wife and I lost a child.

It wasn't a massive awakening, nothing definitive, but none the less a strong strange feeling, enough to jolt the conscious mind, enough to anchor a totally out of the ordinary moment to register something else going on in a moment one would least expect it.

I am not telling this story to gain any sympathy. It may seem sad as you read through, but what I am about to tell you, while perceiving a very painful experience at the time, is when we look back at the event and how it all unfolded it has been nothing but an amazingly beautifully orchestrated experience that I for one had to experience and the evidence of this is that I did experience it.

I felt a moment in time to teach me to become a stronger and better person, a better father and husband because of it.

I actually had no plans for marriage let alone fatherhood, so to better prepare for what our source had in store for me, our source chose a beautiful loving patient woman in my wife for the amazing lesson I was about to receive.

My wife was heavily pregnant with only weeks remaining for full term, we had previously experienced a loss with our first pregnancy, so were anxiously awaiting the arrival of our first child. I was working underground as a miner at the time and my supervisor had called for me to come to the surface, I had no inkling of what was about to unfold.

My supervisor told me I had to go to the hospital immediately as my wife had gone into labour, whilst I knew it was a little early, I knew we were far enough advanced for a successful birth, so there was a mix of excitement and apprehension at the same time.

Upon my arrival at the hospital, it very quickly became evident that there were complications setting in. It wasn't until after the event that I realised what my dear little wife had endured, having to make her way to a neighbour's place seeking help, we couldn't even afford the telephone at the time for many and varied reasons.

As we were living in a fairly remote area, the decision was made to transfer my wife by the flying doctors service to the capital city in our state, and, that I was unable to travel with my wife, I had to drive my vehicle to be with her.

It was during this trip, I had to go what was to be the long road there, as we had to drop the family pet off at my parents' home. As the trip was to take me approximately five or six hours to complete, I had a lot of time to myself, a lot of thinking time, and it was during this trip I experienced my real, noticeable at least "God" or source experience.

As I was motoring along, it was becoming apparent to me, we were in a predicament, as I had no money in the bank, just enough fuel in the car to get me to the parents place and then what?

Where was I going to get the money to get to my wife from my parents' home?

My father and mother were in a financial struggle, I had borrowed to keep a roof over their head, and we were paying off our car as well so with all the outgoing money, we really struggled from one income payment to the next.

It was then that this atheist, blurted out, "God", help me to get through this?

It was weird; I really thought I had no-one or nowhere to turn; the tears of EGO self-pity were beginning to well up within me, and at the same time I had drawn a deep breath, then this feeling of calm seemed to engulf me, I remember it today as clearly as if it happened yesterday, hard to describe but very noticeable I kid you not.

Upon arrival at the parents' home, my mother greeted me at the door, she had just got off the phone, it had been the hospital calling to inform me we had lost the baby, and that my wife had been sedated but was fine for now, our child would be delivered the next day and that I should rest up and head down in the morning.

My head at this time was a swirling blur, my wife needed me, and I wasn't with her, my mother, who was caring for my father at the time as he was dealing with cancer, suggested she come with me the next day.

I couldn't break her heart with the news that I had no money and would have to be sleeping in the car, I would even need to borrow the money for fuel to get there, I mean how bad does it get?

During the evening meal it was then my mother said, "Oh, I forgot to tell you, your tax cheque arrived today!" wow! Some great news in the context of what was happening. The tax cheque was for seven hundred dollars, an amount at that time the equivalent of a month's wages, so quite substantial.

The next morning my mother suggested she come with me to help us through the trauma we were about to experience, my mother, being a nursing sister and a very caring person, a living angel, even wished to pay for the fuel, I gratefully accepted this offer because I knew as soon as I cashed the cheque I could reimburse her, which she was to eventually to decline because of the help she perceived we had given to keep the family home afloat.

Upon arrival at the hospital, we ensured my wife was as comfortable as she could be given circumstances. My mother was to stay with my wife while I went to cash the cheque and arrange accommodation.

Bear in mind, from when I asked, "God" help me to get through this?" we can see synchronicities happening, no money, then the money shows up, my mother offering to pay for the fuel, one may be saying "so what" luck happens, well it goes on.

There were many banking institutions in the city and I selected one nearest the hospital, as you do when you really don't know your way around.

I approached the teller and asked her if she would cash the cheque for me. The teller informed me that cheques must be deposited into an account and it would take three days for it to clear.

I was stunned as to why it would take three days to clear a government cheque, I mean, if this were to bounce then the country would have to be in pretty poor shape wouldn't it?

I explained my predicament and pleaded with the teller with a heartfelt plea, I could see she was genuinely sad and sympathetic toward my plight, but said she was powerless to help me, I am not sure to this day whether she may have pushed a button under the counter, but, right in that moment, the branch manager appeared right on cue.

The bank manager was a gentleman who just happened to be a family friend; we had both grown up in the same little town, been involved in the same sports/football club.

Now what would be the odds of this happening in a city with many banking institutions within it?

My friend Mark saw me and came straight over to say hello and asked what I was up to. When I explained our plight, he immediately turned to the teller and instructed her to honour the cheque which she did, thank you, thank you, thank you.

So while we were going through what we perceived at the time, a very harrowing experience, we were also at the time, although we couldn't see it then being well and truly looked after and cared for, it still sends shivers down my spine when I review it in my mind.

It didn't end there either; we were instructed that because the pregnancy was so far advanced, it was a requirement by law to have a funeral, again something we simply couldn't afford.

I rang the local funeral director and asked if we could pay little by little off a funeral for our child. The funeral director asked if we were covered by private health. We were, so he informed me that private health in those days covered children's funeral costs totally.

And I could go on forever about how the rest of it all fell into place, but I will close off by saying, the question may be asked, well did you ask/attract all these events into your life?

And the answer to that in short is, well yes we did!

Along the way, and only when I look very deeply into the thought patterns of that time, we were continually wondering what could go wrong next. It's sometimes hard to admit it consciously, but once we learn to be totally honest and accountable with ourselves we can see it.

Is there a happy ending to all this? You bet! My beautiful wife and I wished for two children, my wife wished she could have twins so we could get it over in one go, and by now you can guess the rest, yes beautiful twin girls being the end result.

Through our studies, it has been brought to our attention on more than one occasion, that the spirit of the miscarried child remains with the mother for the next opportunity and makes a better go of it, well we miscarried twice, we wanted two, my wife wished for it to happen all at once and it has happened, what more can I say, but thank you, thank you, thank you.

Do the challenges continue?

So has my life change after that episode? Yes it has, life is about continual change, change never stops happening in any part of the universe, if nothing changed there would be no universe.

There will always be challenges in life no-one is exempt. Christ had challenges and today even the Dali Lama has them, the Chinese government exiling him from his own country for what is essentially his belief of what is the truth, it's well documented that governments don't handle the truth very well bless them, and to a lesser extent like missing flights etc.

Mostly we don't understand why things happen until we look back. An example of this is when I was a youngster, a very close friend; really gave me a hiding. We were out driving around and he was drinking very heavily, well there were a few of us in the car at the time.

My friend came up with this idea that we pay a girl a visit and have a sexual liaison with her, the girl had no idea of what was being contemplated for her, in fact she would have been happily at home in the comfort of her bed feeling safe from the world.

My friend suggested we pay her a visit, I knew this person to be of a very good upbringing in a very supportive family, it's fairly traumatic I'd suggest, happening to any person no matter what the upbringing.

Anyway, I wasn't prepared to go along with this and my friends were becoming fairly aggressive and suggested I pull over to the side of the road as they needed to urinate.

Once outside of the car I overheard them discussing dragging me from the car and returning to the home of this innocently sleeping girl, it was around 2.00am.

When I heard this discussion taking place and as we were out in the middle of nowhere, I made the decision there and then to drive off and leave them to walk home and sober up, hopefully arrive at a sensible outcome, contrary to their current thinking.

It disturbed me to think that my friends could be thinking this way; I mean what were they thinking?

Rape, my friend's parents would have been devastated to think their sons and brother could be even thinking this way, I know my closest friend would have potentially murdered anyone for even thinking this way about his sister.

They would have served a gaol sentence; the girl could have chosen, I say chosen, as we have the choice to continually choose thinking or reliving events that have past, and as past events are over and no longer a part of our current lives, may have continued to carry this burden for the rest of her life had it eventuated.

Now sometimes sacrifices are made, my friends ensured they caught up with me at some ungodly hour and belted the living daylights out of me for leaving them on the roadside, my reward for being the saint.

Now, I had the choice to be bitter, and I was for a while, I also sought to seek revenge, I took on martial arts, for all the wrong reasons at the time, but I was soon to learn that proper skilled martial arts is very spiritual if you study its deeper meaning.

The point I am coming to here is, when you look back to the deepest level, you begin to see why all these things happen, and it makes it so much easier to forgive.

One, had I have not driven off when I did, this woman's life may have been shattered, and to this day, she is still blissfully unaware of what was I'd suggest only moments away from what could have been a life shattering experience.

Two, my friend never went to gaol and his family, while they knew something had happened between us, never had to experience the shame of having a violent rapist in their family, his father being a highly respected citizen in the community, would have been devastated to think he had raised a rapist.

The way I see it now, is our source needed to protect the girl from my friends, and to protect my friends from themselves, and knew that I would eventually understand why this all needed to happen which I have, I am so grateful.

I had been selected to protect this lovely woman and these guys who have all turned out to be husbands and fathers in their own right, so thank you, thank you, thank you for being selected to work for the source in an hour of need.

Trust me; I didn't see it that way at the time and what a small price to pay for such an honour.

We all have challenges of one kind and another, but it is sent to help us grow, prosper and strengthen along the way.

We only have to look at the well documented life of the beautiful Oprah Winfrey for an example of someone who has had to overcome adversity and challenges in her life, and she would be the first to acknowledge that she would still have challenges today; she can just overcome them with a little more confidence and style today.

Oprah understands the "Law of Attraction" she has switched onto it, but because of her social conditioning, she still experiences challenges and is continually working on obtaining the "Christ" like thinking, a consciousness of gratitude for everything that shows up in her life on a daily basis be it the perception of good or bad.

One of the difficult things to come to terms with is the fact that if all that "God" created was good, and we are now awakening to the fact that "everything" is created by "God" or our source, or Fred, again it matters not what we call it, then what we perceive as "bad" is only our perception of it.

While I am not suggesting for one moment that what we witnessed during the terrorist act against the twin towers during September 11 was a good thing, to me it was a despicable act, but there were many extremists around the world who thought it was the most wonderful thing to have ever happened.

And likewise, after the Bali bombers were shot by the firing squad for masterminding that attack, there were some among us who saw that as these people getting their just deserts, the firing squad.

We even had people celebrating because of it, now is it right to be on the one hand condemning those people for killing innocent people, and then seeing us as just as joyful upon witnessing their death, who is right and who is wrong?

In the eyes and the minds of their peers, they would be seen as Marta's or Christs' in amongst all the carnage and needless, pointless madness.

It is the terrorists thinking that they are right and this is what they are trained to believe, what Allah requires of them, and at the same time our governments (Australian) spend something to the tune of 30 billion dollars a year to train elite killing machines we call soldiers, send them into the foreign countries on the premise they are protecting our shores from terrorists.

If the other countries were to be sending their soldiers into Australia, there would be a public outcry of terrorism, yet we condone sending our troops entering someone else's turf to kill innocent women and children then sympathetically apologising. In fact we are even training them to efficiently kill/murder their own brothers and sisters then wonder why some of them rebel and shoot our soldiers.

Who are the terrorists?

The terrorists as we see them see us as the terrorists, just as we see them as terrorists, so who is right and who is wrong?

It depends on which side of the fence we are standing on.

And who is good and who is bad? What is good and what is bad? We have murders happening on our streets on a daily basis, but do we label them terrorists?

No it's generally murders, and what if our soldiers kill families by mistake or when they have a brain melt down, oh they were only terrorists anyway!!!... Who can say that? I can't, I wasn't even there, so I would only be plucking a label out of the air.

There is not one child born onto this planet that has an intention to kill another human being, we train them, we socially condition them, every human being arrived here from some kind of act of love, and some may even query all events as an act of love, as there are documented cases of forced sexual abuse, but in its essence one party has a desire for love!

We can label it any way we see fit, but a perception is only a perception.

Personally I totally prefer consensual relationships, but I am just stating facts here, there must be the desire of love from at least one party for a birth to begin taking place, and in most cases the mother will love the child regardless or hand it off to someone who will love the child.

The fact remains, there is not one child born onto this great beautiful planet with an agenda to kill another, it's a learned conditioning, and we spend literally trillions of dollars building weapons and machinery of mass destruction in the name of trying to overcome hatred with acts of hatred, how cleaver is that?

So again one must ask who is right and who is wrong? Who is the terrorist? The Taliban forces or the allied forces, when in the eyes of either party the terrorists are one and the same, whichever way we twist or play with words.

All religious persuasions have the "thou shall not kill" rule, so where does it say "with the exception of?"

I have read and also heard somewhere that during the war crimes investigations former German soldier stated that "it's easy for leaders to create war, they just have to tell the dumb farmers they/we are being attacked and they will take up arms and go to war believing they're protecting and serving their country!"

And we have evidence of this today, we have sent troops over to Vietnam to kill and be killed, there are returned soldiers around today who still do not understand why they were sent there, they just shrug their shoulders and say "I don't know, because we had too when our marble dropped!" how sad is that?

Today we have troops in Afghanistan killing and being killed, and when they're killed our perceived leaders stand up and say "he/she was killed in the line of duty, defending our shores!"

They're not defending our shores, they're invading another country and killing their citizens, and how long will it be before their citizens become sick of it and then begin invading our shores?

Then our soldiers will be defending our shores!

I can say without any shadow of doubt, that if I cross into someone else's back yard and start beating up on a family member, even if it were being perceived that I had every right to by the family members, if I keep it up, especially if the family believes I have handed out sufficient punishment, eventually as the blood runs thicker than water, they will surely turn, retaliate and it will escalate until someone is man enough to stand up and forgive.

Again, the great Nelson Mandela is one such powerful example of what I am saying here.

People will only attack another out of fear, there is no exception I am sorry, why must one carry a gun if he doesn't fear for his/her life?

And if they kill another in a foreign country, we bring them home and sing their praises, give them a medal for being brave. I am not saying for one moment that our soldiers aren't wonderful citizens of our country, they are, but eventually they are going to come home and like the Vietnam veterans and those of all the other wars before them, are going to start wondering why all this carnage had to take place and why they were a part of it.

Its only when we choose to look back into history for the true meaning, who invaded who in the first place to find a meaning and realise the only way to stop any war is not with killing more people, but by beginning to have the courage of a Nelson Mandela to forgive those who were perceiving themselves to be in the places of power for all the wrong reasons, for they have no power, they are just frightened people employing others to do their fighting for them, and countries falling into line behind the perceived super powers because they are even more frightened.

The way to remove the challenges from our lives is to align ourselves with the truth, and with the truth then comes the power to achieve anything and that power, flows through each and every one of us there are no exceptions, I feel you will now be beginning to understand what I am saying.

Now would be a good time to put this book down and begin digesting this information. We are all one entity, a spirit having a human experience and not as we are brought up to believe, human beings having a spiritual experience

How did I discover "The Law of Attraction"?

Well again, I used to be very sceptical, so can understand why people who are sceptical, take some shifting from this conscious mindset.

You see with the **"Law of Attraction"** the more love you give, the more love you receive back, the same with money, the more money you give, the more you receive back.

It is very important to note, if you only give to receive, the chances are we will miss the returns, because it doesn't always return the exact same way, amount or circumstance as what we give, so it is easy to miss the return.

At the same time, if we give hatred, we receive back more of the same, we get angrier because of it, and the **emotion** becomes stronger, so we draw even greater things to make us angrier and it escalates again war is a glaring example of this.

Therefore, for the sceptic, surely he is going to attract to himself, people, events and circumstances that will prove their point, we get what we have our attention upon every time.

So it took some time, a very long time in fact, for me to come to the realisation of it, and even today, I sometimes have my doubts because of many years of past conditioning and so attract events and circumstances confirming my doubts, but I catch myself out more easily these days.

An example of this, I spoke earlier about a guy with "no arms and no legs" Nick Vujicic, I was explaining this to some work colleagues of mine, showed them the "you tube video", and of course it can be very **emotional** seeing the tears of love streaming down the cheeks of his seminar participants, not to become overcome with **emotion** also.

The very next day, I visited a small town on business, after completing the business I called into a little café on the outskirts of town for a cappuccino.

Entering the café, right before me stood a man with no arms, how many people do we see around the place with no arms?

Today I can link the **"The Law of Attraction"** pretty much too any area of my life.

When I was a sceptic, my first response to a story like that would be, "so what! What does that prove?

But not anymore, I have too much evidence, just the same as when I was a sceptic, I had all of the evidence then as well to say it didn't exist, as do I have as much evidence today to say that, yes it does exist.

So for me it really didn't happen overnight and as I suggest, and it is essentially as our conscious mind cannot or will not comprehend or give credence to anything we cannot see.

Even though we can't see electricity, we know it's there, because we are now programmed or hard wired into our brain from birth that it's there so we don't ever give it a second thought.

We can't see radio waves either, but again we are hard wired from birth to have some understanding of it.

Again television signals are all around us, but we don't give it much thought, we don't even realise that all these transmissions are flowing right through us where ever we are.

I've tried to explain this and because we are not taught this at school, it can'l bo right, so when I do try to explain this, even with a visual, portable television, or with an iPhone, some still think I am loopy.

I don't take it personally, in fact I see it as a compliment, as most of the "out there thinkers" were all loopy weren't they?

Gee Darrell Poke was in my class at school and he was dumb he he...

We all have perceptions, excuses, labels and beliefs and that's fine, but I am totally comfortable where I sit, as I am not alone with what I am saying right now.

I have learned from many and varied teachers who at the same time as you are reading this, are also teaching millions of other people across the planet right now, you are only seeing my perspective of it, seeing it from a different point of view but with a similar outcome.

Living life in auto pilot

Initially I blundered my way through life, from one experience to the next, and also from one highlight to the next, the saying "when you're on a roll, you're on a roll" rings so true.

Then doubt creeps in, because we begin saying, how long is this going to last? Or "I had better make the most of this while it lasts" so we are subconsciously preparing ourselves for the down fall or the luck to come to an end, and as sure as the sun rises every day, it does come to an end, because we *"attracted"* it sadly, so that's how it is while we remain on auto pilot.

When things are beginning to go wrong, we make statements like "what can go wrong next?"

Then we're consciously looking for something to go wrong, ask and you will receive!

But I didn't ask for that we say, so no you didn't ask for that, we were just thinking about what could go wrong and got what we thought about.

Like everyone else, I fluctuate with the mixed results and still do, listen to this statement, "I find it difficult to find people who understand me!"

What am I asking unconsciously "can I have people who can't understand me?" and boy oh boy, weren't they showing up, and of cause the more frustrated I became, the greater the numbers started showing up.

Initially yes it was frustratingly slow for me, I became somewhat reclusive for a while and practiced affirmations to help change the mindset a little, I backed off trying to excitedly explain all my luck to people around me, until I managed to **"attract"** like-minded people.

I did some of this by putting my perspective of the political arena by sending letters into a local newspaper and listening to the feedback generated from giving my perspective.

The feedback started as a trickle at first, now wherever I go, people come up to me in the street, some to offer their opinion, have a discussion about my point of view etc. and now some people tell me they only buy the paper and scan the letters to the editor to see if I have a letter in before they read anything else, or ask me if I have anymore going in soon.

From writing comments to a local newspaper I have **attracted** quite a following and from what I've learned from some amazing teachers, and from people from all walks of life, its gradually emerging for me as someone who has evolved from an academic failure to someone who's opinion is respected.

Only because I am **"Awakening"** to what I am understanding to be the truth.

I could say that I cruised along on auto pilot for the first thirty (30) years through perceptions of good luck, followed by bad luck, until I eventually became a union representative, the training of becoming a union representative didn't sit very well with me, because it was all about manipulating the minds of others to achieve results I/the union wanted.

I guess it didn't sit too well with me simply because it was all about controlling the masses, like always asking the group first to vote on what I wished to achieve as most people respond to the first motion, the question was always to be structured "all those for" or "all those against" whichever way you wished the amendment to go and it always had to be a show of hands, no secret ballot as people may truly reflect what they wished and it may not be how I/we wanted it to pan out.

If someone moved a motion, that didn't reflect what you desired, it would always be along the lines of "what idiot wishes to second that stupid motion?"

No-one wants to be seen as the idiot or stupid, so generally no-one would second the motion whether they thought it were a good suggestion or otherwise, if they did, then one would have to sigh and roll the eyes in the back of the head as if this were a silly waste of time, negative body language, and then it would be "those against?"

The hands would go up, some would be a little hesitant at first as they would be feeling it was right to vote for, but waited for others to raise their hand first before they themselves did so.

Remember from EGO conscious no-one wishes to look stupid, and as we are conditioned from an early age, always put clean undies on before you go out, you wouldn't want to have an accident and be caught with dirty undies now would you?

The chances are, we're probably going to wet or crap our self during the accident anyway, and the health professionals are going to be more concerned about our life threatening injuries than discussing the state of our undies.

But this is how we are unconsciously conditioned as we grow up and it still goes on in adulthood, all these false beliefs we instil into our children, and I am just as guilty for blue printing it into the minds of my children, it's been handed down from generation to generation right through history to now, but now, the ship is turning.

So I was not sitting really comfortable manipulating the truth to the advantage of taking advantage of an employee or an employer, and having said this, there were and possibly still are today, employers who take advantage of their employees, so I could see the need for a negotiator for those who feel they're not educated enough to be a constructive negotiator, that is ask their manager for better working conditions so we could be a better employee for them.

And at the same time, there are employees who tako advantage of their employer, but once we realise that one cannot reach ultimate productivity without the other and begin to **harmonise and work as one**.

The whole world could work together to help farm and feed each other, help construct dwellings for the perceived less fortunate, starvation and poverty would cease to exist.

I could see the need for unions, and was happy to represent the masses, but again was very uncomfortable about the manipulation of others for basically my own benefits, for me it had to be a win for the worker and a win for the manager a harmonious outcome if we were to survive.

Questioning the truth

I questioned the hierarchy about these archaic methods of resolution and was falling out of favour with them for doing so, this also leads me into questioning other behaviour, and so unconsciously I began *"attracting"* evidence of other unruly behaviour to the point of criminal activity going on with the funding from members money.

It's a long story, but fast forward, I subsequently left the employment, made redundant actually and finished up working within the mining industry.

Three months into my new employment and happily resigned from the union rife with criminal activity, a decision was made by the members of the union involved at the mine, to change unions because of dissatisfaction from the union at the mine site.

One can hazard a guess as to which union the miners were wishing to cross over too, that being the union I was previously embroiled in, so with *the emotion of hate* for this union rife with criminal activity, here they were knocking on the door of my new employer, I was questioning what I had done to deserve this, but was unknowingly *"attracting"* this very union into my new workplace.

Having only been working there for three months, many of the miners had not yet got to know me, so when I refused to re-join a union I knew had criminal activists within it, tensions become strained, my head was telling me not to rock the boat, but my heart was telling me, for the benefit of the workforce and the community at large, I had better hold my ground.

It wasn't a real good time for the company either, as the metal prices were very low and the cost of hauling the ground out for processing had become very costly, the mine had been closed, recently restructured how they were going about things.

Originally I had only taken the job interview as an opportunity to gain valuable interview experience for a job in another location as I had a small family to house, clothe and feed.

I had no real desire to enter the mining industry at that time, even though my previous job had me working underground in power producing construction and nothing to do with minerals extraction.

Ultimately as it is evident, I was offered a position within the mine, I felt an obligation by not wasting their time and accepted the position with them.

It became quickly evident that this place was struggling to produce and make ends meet, most of the miners who remained were still very bitter with the restructuring and felt they had been let down by their union.

I tried to tell them at this time, it's better the devil you know than the devil you don't as the union they were involved in, while not standing in line for saint hood, the union they were wishing to exchange to had very corrupt elements within it, which I knew was still present as they were still appearing at the site trying to woo the membership.

Enter the visionary life changer

At this time, my head was spinning as to what to do, and as if right on cue, the general manager resigned and the incoming manager, South African Mr Richard Scallan a man with truly amazing insights, phenomenal past achievements, and a very cheery, very, very can do attitude.

Mr Scallan had been employed by the company as a trouble shooter for failing sections of the business, to either build them up to a saleable standard or to make it a profitable one.

Mr Scallan had an amazing capacity for digesting information, identifying strengths and weaknesses and had very soon set about rectifying things among and amidst all the union unrest an old mine running at massive losses to the tune of what equated to around a million dollars a month.

Many of the miners were hard wired/conditioned in their old ways and were proving very hard to shift to new ways of thinking.

Enter my first exposure to the *"new"* way of thinking, well not new in its essence, it should read, the forgotten way of thinking.

The program introduced by Mr Scallan, a program called **"Investment in Excellence"** developed by an organization called The Pacific Institute and its founder a wonderful person and one of the fathers of positive thinking during my time, Mr Lou Tice.

Now this stuff to me, at first, seemed pretty weird and with religious overtones, remember, being raised Atheist and a very uneducated sceptic it was bound to raise eyebrows and some confusion within the **"super computer"** we have all been lovingly and freely fitted out with (our brain), as my virus riddled programming was beginning to go into overload, sometimes freezing the screen of reality for me.

But none the less, this was to be the beginning of the first tusto of this quantum shift.

Richard Scallan was and still to this day, is a very heavily religious man, but a kind and loving man, some didn't see him this way though, and sometimes Mr Scallan needed to deliver some tough love, of which I wasn't exempt either.

It could have easily been construed that this man was a hard uncompromising man, but he was given the task to turn things around, so sometimes tough love was to be dished out to help us move or wake up.

Tough love

On one such occasion a young miner had been dismissed from the site for threatening behaviour toward another miner, and the members were informed by their union that they could take the dismissal to court, but the chance of reinstatement of the young miner were very slim because of the nature of the incident, it was the companies duty to protect its workforce from harm of any nature.

I was eventually asked if I would speak with Mr Scallan and the management team about having the young man reinstated, and as it turned out, I did.

No-one, not even the miner threatened in this incident wished to see anyone lose their job, but what transpired between the management team and myself wasn't going to be a very nice experience for me either.

My position within the company was also to be placed on the line if this young man were to reoffend, but having been in a similar position at a similar age, only I had actually punched my boss, this young man had only threatened another employee.

Long story short, I challenged the positive program in that we were told to see windows of opportunity and take them.

The young man had to go home, sit at the end of the table at mealtime with his wife and two little children and explain his actions to them, no job, no income, a lesson for him that hatred doesn't put food upon the table.

Having previously been through similar circumstances, I had an opportunity to pass my lesson on, which I did.

Right in that point of time, I, being one man, I didn't realise then but do now, that in that particular moment, I had more power working with me, than the whole of the union movement who were rendered helpless by their conditioned inflexibility.

I am not bragging about this, to do so would be going straight to the EGO, and that's not what this is about, this is about being able to open up to working with our higher consciousness, something we all have access to.

So by the past event, I began to utilise the **"power of positive thinking"** to achieve seemingly impossible tasks into achievable things.

Again I am humbled by that event and to have had the opportunity to help someone else from the lessons of life I have had making it even more rewarding.

At the same time passing on my life experiences, if a reader of this book can draw some similarities or parallels from what I am saying right now then we are both in for an excellent time as neither of us has wasted our time.

Again, Mr Scallan is a religious man and I prefer to by-pass the middle man (religion) and make direct contact with **head office** which is something we unconsciously all do any way even if religious, atheist or just by being spiritual, its following intuition and not the direction or orders of some organised group which are also a part of the bigger picture.

The way it is meant to be for whatever the reason we can only ever know when we choose to look back, who are we to question the motives behind the organising energy or **"our higher self"**.

Life takes a different direction

Early one morning while readying myself for work, I switched the television on, and here was this massive mountain of a man spruiking *"YOU CAN CHANGE YOUR LIFE IN AN INSTANT, CREATE THE LIFE OF YOUR DREAMS! BUY MY PROGRAM AND I WILL TELL YOU HOW!"* enter one of the leading life coachs on the planet today **Anthony Robbins.**

Anthony Robbins is a world renowned life coach, a man with a passion and an endless energy, a very loving and amazing person.

I once quipped, "This bloke is filling in for Christ until he returns!"

But when we get to the realisation that there is no beginning and no end to anything, it soon becomes evident that Christ has never left at all, but that's another story in its-self.

I had actually unconsciously **"attracted"** Tony's program, and hopefully this will become more evident as we progress, but will continue with how this awakening happens for me.

I was following Tony's program with mixed results, (A) because while I thought I was following Tony's program to the letter of the **"law"** I have since found out that I wasn't, and it was a combination of reasons why, and one of those was, when Tony used to say **"you must commit to this for thirty days!"** I thought I did commit for thirty days but probably over a forty or fifty day period having lay day gaps in between.

I mean, I did thirty days' worth with a little break here and there, like taking the kids to sports etc. not realising that it really needed to be a continuous thirty day period without a break, which I have since discovered, **"when asking"** I wonder why these programs aren't working for me?

I *"attracted"* the answer from another program of **Jack Canfield of the "chicken soup for the soul books" and the DVD "The Secret" fame**, where Jack explained, you must follow this program for thirty days continuously, **_and here's the reason why!_** Aaaaaahhh, the reason why!!!

Jack explains that NASA had discovered it took astronauts a minimum of thirty days to get accustomed to weightlessness, it took thirty days for the subconscious mind to accept the different conditions, I now understand why the astronauts used to struggle to walk after a week or a fortnight spent in outer space, their brain was in the middle of a transitional phase.

N.A.S.A. have developed goggles that when worn, trick/train the subconscious mind into similar simulated circumstances astronauts experience when in outer space experiencing weightlessness.

Much the same as international airline pilots can experience most every scenario they may encounter during flights, or formula one race drivers have simulator training before each event to better prepare them for the race, such are the critical aspects of making the correct decisions within a split second which is crucial to them winning and staying alive while travelling at neck breaking speeds.

The thirty days must be completed in consecutive days NASA discovered.

If the trainee removed the goggles, say 20 or 25 days into the program, it wouldn't work and the next day had to begin again as day one and be continued for the full thirty days consecutively for the subconscious mind to totally accept it as fact!

This is very critical for it to work for any new program, even learning to drive a car as well I'd suggest.

So while Tony's teachings are/were spot on for reaching success, there was one critical aspect I could find or subconsciously overlooked in it, was the fact that Tony may have assumed, I had his drive and passion to commit for thirty days, and I did, but I didn't see the relevance or the importance of missing a day or two here and there would have, but I do now Tony, please forgive my ignorance.

Introduction to Wayne W Dyer

Anthony Robbins's program also involved receiving a bonus monthly CD coaching called **"Power talk"** where Tony did interviews with leading life coaches that he has studied with along his path to enlightenment.

And there was one such interview with a gentleman by the name of **Dr Wayne W Dyer** who at the time, I thought "he's an interesting fellow", I resonated with his calm manner and powerful teaching presence, and what a bonus Dr Dyer's teachings have turned out to be.

I dutifully rushed down to the local book store to see if they had any copies of this gentleman's work in stock, and they did, just one book which I now know without any shadow of doubt, was sitting patiently on the shelf waiting for me to arrive and purchase it.

It was the only book of Dr Dyer's the store had after initially being told they had never heard of the man.

This was to be a real **"awakening"** experience for me.

As I got into the first chapter Dr Dyer suggested I put this book down, go back to my earliest child hood memory, and slowly think through the events of my life that come to mind, basically putting it into five year chunks, and then I would come to the realisation as to why I had picked this book up.

The clarity that hit me is very hard to describe, it was as if this person knew me.

The next chapter was even more interesting, which basically said "and the part you are now going to struggle with for a little while, is, the fact that your life was planned/mapped out before you even come here in the physical.

Before I actually chose to become a human being?

Now this was really weird, because quite frankly I don't recall making any plans to becoming a human being, in fact I still can't recall doing this, but the more I am learning the more it is beginning to make some sense, but more about that later.

So with, the *"Investment with excellence"* program stimulating my subconscious mind, I *"attracted"* Anthony Robbins, and from there, *"attracted"* Dr Wayne W Dyer who happens to be very close to a **Dr Deepak Chopra**, then came *"The Secret"* by Australia's Rhonda Byrne which contains many of the world's leading spiritual coaches and a list too long to mention them all.

While I do mention all these spiritual/life coaches, it must be made aware; I do not work for any of them.

So am not advertising their books/programs, I do endorse them otherwise I wouldn't have mentioned them, and I also must stress at this point, none of them have endorsed this book either.

It would be an honour if any of them did but I am sure I have their blessing by acknowledging my effort to follow their path to enlightenment and effort to making our world a much, much nicer place for all of us to dwell in.

Reviewing what we have learned

If I could start winding down for now, I am sure for those who are well into their journey of enlightenment, would find my journey reassurance that they are not on their path alone, and possibly find it refreshing to see things from my perspective.

Also, I do realise that there are others who are just setting out on their journey who will need time to digest everything they have just read and are reading.

There will be many questions to ask, and can I say this, as I stated very early within this book, we are learning until we take our last breath, as I discovered while being fortunate enough to be with my father at the time he returned to source energy.

I say fortunate enough as not everyone gets to have that moving experience with those who cross back by what we perceive accidental death.

I really need to write a book about the next phase of life from my perspective; I am so comfortable with it all now. The book will be called "Death, Fact or Fallacy"

My father demonstrated to me without question, only hours before crossing back that he was still capable of learning something new.

So don't become frustrated at the pace of how things unfold, as frustration attracts more things to be frustrated about.

It's a process of developing a belief then onto a knowing, and then it comes down to developing pure faith.

As you may now understand, I/we have been through some real challenges along the way, character building yes, but as I am writing this, I am 100% healthy, am totally fine, a few scars yes, mother earth supports scars also, but is still functioning beautifully, has done for billions of years and who knows, will do so for billions of years to come, contrary to what pessimists may say, at the end of the day, we are evolving as a species.

OK, we have ascertained by the stubby process that we struggle to find a starting point for the bottle, bearing in mind, the ingredients for the glass has been around, and was around for the caveman to utilise, but he hadn't yet evolved to do so, so it's fair to say it was possibly around prior to the caveman.

We can't be certain of the beginning, there is the big bang theory, but it's a theory as yet and some metaphysicians believe the big bang theory is mathematically impossible and that the universe is actually expanding and contracting.

The entire ingredient for the beer, as we know is seasonal, so has been harvested since when?

By how many farmers hop pickers etc.?

And when will all this end? There is no given date.

The actual beer or content where does that end?

Yep it enters the body, but then what happens, does it end there?

We process the water, filter that out and pass in our urine/perspiration, again sorry for being blunt, but I am just stating facts here! and as we know the urine ends up where?

Back into the ocean via sewerage systems or onto the ground, again who knows?

The sun's rays draw the water from the earth only to be re-deposited somewhere else at some other time, who knows, maybe back at the brewery.

The rest of the beer/content ingredient is utilised as energy within our bodies, turned into blood, and later removed as waste matter, which is returned to the earth eventually, and is utilised as it breaks down from its physical form into nutrients for the earth as insect/bacterium/plant food, the whole cycle continually revolves around in never ending circles and cycles.

All the machinery and equipment to move the ingredient for the stubby and the final product, is made from metal, which was once just a mineral contained within the earth, again all this was sitting there patiently awaiting man to evolve.

The ever evolving human, has and always will evolve from something as simple as a thought!

Who would believe?

But everything has begun with a thought, even us, our parents thought romance, so it is also conceivable that we chose the moment to come here to have the human experience.

Although we probably can't remember making this choice, it's becoming more evident by the day that we are **"Spirit"** having the **"Human"** experience rather than what we were lead to believe, that being in most cases, a **"Human being"** having a **"Spiritual"** experience.

So if this is the case, then we must have made the choice to come here when we did and I suspect all will be revealed soon enough as we continue to evolve.

I sit very comfortable with it all now, but assure you, at first, as I began to experience an awakening; it was as I perceived it at the time, a very mentally challenging experience.

I would suggest in a metaphoric way, like starting out in a new career, or leaving school and having to earn a living, set up a home, having bills coming in, all things we took for granted as our parents used to do it all for us, now we had to make those decisions on our own.

At first, it all may have been very daunting or challenging, but like learning to drive a motor vehicle we soon acclimatise and it all becomes second nature.

Hence the repetition of a lot of the material I am presenting to you now, by reading/hearing things multiple times, our subconscious mind becomes more accepting of it as with any learning, and it's all about repetition, ask any sports person who is at the top of their game.

It is also scientifically proven, any person who practices in their mind, over and over a task like shooting a basketball through the hoop, as we think in pictures, we picture the ball dropping through the basket from any angle/distance, if we do this daily for *"thirty days"* even without actually physically touching a basketball, the results are phenomenal.

Seeing results

I suggest by now, you have been making some comparisons from what you have read, to some of your own life experiences, or correlate what you have read with other material you have observed through the many media outlets available to us today.

But it is all a truth ingrained within us, so we recognise it as we are attracting it, again, our EGO mind will do its darnedest to reject it, and this part of our mind is what religion refer to as the devil.

The best way to see results is do as most material I suggest, start by trying something small, place your attention upon something as we suggested when we get the new car, we then see similar vehicles everywhere, and see how often it appears.

It is massively important, that once we have asked, we must then shift our focus upon expectation of what we asked for arriving; remove all doubt of it happening.

If we keep asking for the same thing over and over, it's telling **"our higher self"** we don't have it yet, so it won't materialise for us, developing this trust in the beginning can be challenging for some, as it is for me, but remember, the more we put in, the more we get back.

If the glass is half full, there is room for negative energy to get in, so the more of whatever we put in, it will begin to flow out, the doubt will subside and be replaced with absolute trust.

Develop an **"attitude of gratitude"** again, as I've explained with some of the perceived challenges of life I have personally dealt with, it was only when I looked back, could I see how it all unfolded.

I then had to make the choice to follow my EGO mind and continually live in sorrow and self-pity, or make the choice to work out the reason, look for the positives within it to appreciate why it actually happened.

As with the time I was beaten up for choosing not to participate in a moment of sexual gratification with my friends, today the lovely lady is a blissfully happy grandparent, my friends families never had to live with the stigma of raising a rapist.

I now am honoured to have been chosen to intervene in what could have perceived to devastate so many wonderful families. *So thank you, thank you, and thank you!*

It matters not our circumstances, we can very quickly turn them around, by changing the way we think about things, the things we think about change.

Again, there are many, many programs that I could recommend, but we will attract what works best for us, I have attracted many amazing teachers along my journey, and while each one has an awesome value and a method to assist in helping change happen, and generally like in my case, have all had their own Aaaaahhhh, moments in their own way.

I would have I suggest, spent many thousands of dollars on purchasing programs and books to pass onto family and friends excitedly to allow them to have my experience, and it simply hasn't worked for them in the same way it did for me.

Master life coach Anthony Robbins, stresses this point, he cannot make another rich!!

I now fully understand what he is saying, **"we cannot think for another person"** and therefore cannot do it for them, example; I could give someone a million dollars, and they would be euphoric for a while, feel rich, and then something might happen, tax office catches up with them, it could be anything, all of a sudden, they would feel as if they are losing their new found wealth, very soon, that's exactly what happens, it disappears.

They put it down to bad luck, greedy others taking it from them and the list goes on, not fully realising they actually attracted it to themselves, they probably end up even in a worse position than before they had the million dollars and then label money as evil because of the experience, and it all reverts back generally to earlier child hood neurological social conditioning.

Personally I have been lead to an amazing teacher, thankfully who teaches self-hypnosis, Dr Robert Anthony, who explains in the very simplistic terms, how we can use a program he has developed to use self-hypnosis, enter the subconscious mind and reprogram it to become more connected and receptive to our higher self, or as he puts it, our ESP our **"Essential Silent Partner"** and it is essential, as without it, nothing exists!!!

Dr Anthony explains the one brain, two minds metaphor as the conscious mind being the captain of the ship, who gives the orders/directions, to the subconscious mind being the crew, who diligently carry out the orders it receives.

He then goes on to explain, there is the gate keeper, or I'd suggest in this case purser who ensures all directions are followed to standard, what we are programmed to do, and it really won't change directions from anything the captain offers even if it can see the captain has erred in the decision making on this occasion.

So we need to get past the gate keeper, in order to reprogram the crew to avert disaster, and this is where self-hypnosis comes into play, it diverts the attention of the gatekeeper long enough to reprogram the crew.

A little like installing an anti-virus program into a computer to help get it functioning properly only the computer we are programming is far greater than anything man made and quite possibly will ever make.

Another example of what we are capable of, something I had a massive amount of doubt about achieving but did.

Anthony Robbins has an event program called **"Unleash the Power Within"** which my wife and I attended.

During this program, Tony offers participants the opportunity to perform the traditionally Fijian fire walk experience, where each participant is encouraged to write something they wish to release themselves from, screw it up and throw it into a fire and realise that this was their past, and the past is exactly that. "Let it go and get rid of it".

Sometime later the participants are encouraged to remove their shoes and socks/stockings and stroll six meters in bare feet across the burning embers. The embers which have been burning all day, are around 1200deg, we cook a pig at 400deg, and all who wish to participate walk across the embers and wipe their feet on moist grass on the other side, to my amazement, not even a blister.

How are we able to manage this?

Well I put it down to the fact, as we have to place ourselves into a trance like state before attempting to walk across the flaming embers, once the higher-self realises we are serious about doing this, it sends all the resources to our feet, we profusely begin perspiring through the soles of our feet, thus protecting the skin from burning, such is the power we have working within to protect us from harm if we can by-pass the gatekeeper **ego mind**, who is essentially there to protect us from harm, and is pre-programmed from our social conditioning.

You may very well be asking, well what does walking on fire prove?

What it does demonstrate is, that from our pre-programming our EGO or gate keeper will tell us, **"don't do that stupid, you will get burned and hospitalised!"** This in essence, is true.

But if we connect to our higher self, place our trust in it we then find, it becomes a lie, as we can not only walk safely across the fire, we can do so without getting burned or hospitalised.

So while the gate keeper does protect us, it also holds us back from being able to work with our higher self, it instils false doubt as to what we are actually capable of.

So what Dr Anthony offers with his program, is the opportunity, to slip past the gatekeeper and re-program the crew to allow us to achieve and believe we are truly capable of unlimited possibilities, of which we all are, there are no exceptions, again, if a man with no arms and no legs can find amazing love, happiness and prosperity in life, then where does it leave us perceived able bodied people with our perceived hardship and challenges?

Is Nick Vujicic just lucky he is the way he is?

Or has he just changed the perception of how he sees himself and make the most of what he's got?

Nick Vujicic, has made a personal choice to choose to see himself as our "Sources" perfect creation, something of which each and every one of us are, and utilise his (some may perceive) imperfections.

Understand we all have this choice to love who we are, to love each other, be grateful for the air we breathe, which is the perceived waste given off from the tree's, oxygen and the trees gratefully receive the waste we give off, being carbon dioxide, urine water with minerals and nutrients, and our faeces, another source of perceived human waste which is in essence food and nutrient for soil and other life forms.

Plants sustain bacterium life, another biological universe which we cannot see with the naked eye, but which is such an integral part of the magnificence of the entire universe as we know it is a living mass of vibrational connected energy, all moving at many and varying speeds and frequencies.

Again, there will be people who will challenge the validity of my own personal "Spirituality" and that is fine, while I am being questioned, it helps me to search for the truth in my own mind for the answers, so in essence help me to becoming the better person I am striving to become.

At the end of the day, I only have myself to answer to, and what another person thinks of me is truly none of my business.

As long as I am kind to others and happy within myself, make my contribution to the betterment of mankind and the planet along the way, then I have served my time during my human experience within this existence and that's all that really matters.

Like those great contributors before, I can only be grateful for the likes of the Wright brothers for helping humanity fly around the world, so I will not be complaining if I miss my next flight, it all happens for a reason.

I will not complain during the next power failure, because I can be grateful for Benjamin Franklin, not allowing the ridicule of the masses for their perception of him being weird for having a notion he could harness energy.

I will not complain, the next time a light bulb blows, when I can be grateful Thomas Edison didn't listen to the masses telling him to give up trying to replace candle light with a light bulb, even when he failed one thousand times.

The experts of the day knew in their own minds, that what he was trying to achieve was impossible, I mean, his experiment did fail one thousand times didn't it?

I will not complain the next time my car breaks down (if it ever does) because the likes of Henry Ford believed we could get around in an automobile and take the burden from horse draw drays, even the wheel made it easier for the horses, so I can be grateful for that can't I?

I will finish off with some magic potions from successful people, I choose to use in my daily life.

Wisdom of Mother Theresa

1. People are often unreasonable, illogical and self-centred, "forgive them anyway!"
2. If you are kind, people may accuse you of selfish ulterior motives, "Be kind anyway!"
3. If you are successful, you will win some false friends and some true enemies, "Be kind anyway!"
4. If you are honest and frank, people may cheat you, "Be honest and frank anyway!"
5. What you spend years building; people may destroy overnight, "Build anyway!"
6. If you find serenity and happiness, people may become jealous, "Be happy and serine anyway!"
7. The good you do today, people will often forget tomorrow, "Do good anyway!"
8. Give the world the best you have, and it may never be enough, "give the world the best you have any way!"

You see in the final analysis, it's all between you and God, it was never between you and them anyway!

There is so much wisdom and truth in what Mother Theresa says, we never see a bird sitting around complaining, running to the lawyer when its nest has been destroyed, it just builds again, if not in the same location, it will build again because it does as nature intended it to do.

The prayer of St Francis

Lord makes me an instrument of thy peace?

Where there is hatred, let me sow love!

Where there is injury, pardon!

Where there is doubt, faith!

Where there is despair, hope!

Where there is darkness, light!

Where there is sadness, joy!

Oh divine master, grant that I may not so much seek to be consoled, as to console!

To be understood as to understand!

To be loved as to love!

For it is in giving that we receive, and it is in dying to self, that we are born to eternal life.

Amen

Affirmations

I send blessings to everyone and everything in my past. I have benefitted from all that I have experienced.

What I have gone through has brought wonderful lessons, which have made me the person I am today.

I can now leave the past behind me, and release it all to our source energy "God"

I have genius inside and flowing through me continually at all times, I shall ask it questions, and easily, hear, see and find the answers; I can take action in faith and confidence immediately.

When I want something bad enough, I will be shown a way, if I don't want it bad enough, I will find an excuse.

I will always keep my head, when others around me are seemingly losing theirs and I will come through unscathed.

I will always have patience with myself;

I am learning and growing every day, even when I am not consciously aware of my progress.

As I look back on this period of my life, I'll understand how all the pieces fit together.

I will see the blessings and the lessons I have gained from this period of time.

At times I have and can be too hard upon myself.

I've come such a long way and yet, I have been known to chastise myself for not going far or fast enough. So on this day, the message is to have patience with myself and the process of life. All things are divinely timed, just as a flower unfurls its petals, or the fruit on the tree ripens at precisely the right moment, so too does the progress of my life in a perfect timeline.

If I try to force the flower with my hands it would soon wither and die, as surely as if I pick the fruit too early, it would make me feel ill, or taste sour, and so it is with life.

The more I learn to become patient with the progression of life, the more I open the energetic doorways for all the good I could ever imagine, to come to me!

I am patient with myself, I surrender all struggles and the need to control or force things to happen, I happily embrace the knowledge that everything I desire is mine to enjoy.

Amen

Don't quit poem

When things go wrong, and they sometimes will,

When the road you're trudging seems all uphill,

When the funds are low and the debts are high,

When the care is pressing you down a bit, rest if you must, but do not quit.

Life seems queer with its twists and turns,

As everyone sometime learns, and many a failure turns about,

When he might have won had he stuck it out;

Don't give up though the pace seems slow, you may succeed with another blow,

Often the goal is nearer than it seems to a faint and faltering man,

Often the struggler has given up,

When he might have captured the victors' cup,

And he learned too late when the night dipped down,

How close he was to the victors' crown.

Success is a failure turned inside out,

The silver tint of the clouds of doubt.

And you never can tell how close you are; it may be near when it seems so far,

So stick to the fight when your hardest hit, it's when things seem worst, that you must not quit!

Author Unknown